ANSWERING JIHAD

ANSWERING JIHAD

A Better Way Forward

NABEEL QURESHI

ZONDERVAN

Answering Jihad
Copyright © 2016 by Nabeel Qureshi

This title is also available as a Zondervan ebook.
Visit www.zondervan.com/ebooks.

This title is also available as a Zondervan audio book.
Visit www.zondervan.com/fm.

Requests for information should be addressed to:

Zondervan, 3900 *Sparks Dr. SE, Grand Rapids, Michigan 49546*

Library of Congress Cataloging-in-Publication Data

Names: Qureshi, Nabeel, author.
Title: Answering Jihad : a better way forward / Nabeel Qureshi.
Description: Grand Rapids : Zondervan, 2016.
Identifiers: LCCN 2016002811 | ISBN 9780310531388 (softcover)
Subjects: LCSH: Jihad. | Islam--Religious aspects--Christianity. | Christianity
    and other religions--Islam. | Missions to Muslims.
Classification: LCC BP182 .Q74 2016 | DDC 297.7/2--dc23 LC record available at
    http://lccn.loc.gov/2016002811

Any Internet addresses (websites, blogs, etc.) and telephone numbers in this
book are offered as a resource. They are not intended in any way to be or imply
an endorsement by Zondervan, nor does Zondervan vouch for the content of
these sites and numbers for the life of this book.

Published in association with the literary agency of Mark Sweeney and
associates, Naples, Florida, 34113

Cover imagery: Getty Images
Interior design: Matthew Van Zomeren and Ben Fetterley

Printed in the United States of America

16 17 18 19 20 21 22 23 24 25 /DHV/ 15 14 13 12 11 10 9 8 7 6 5 4 3 2 1

THIS BOOK IS DEDICATED TO MY SISTER.

Baji, I miss how close we were in our childhood, even playing with your My Little Ponies and hearing you rave about the Backstreet Boys. You are the most loving sister a younger brother could ask for. I pray that your love for people would extend into a love for truth. I am begging God for the day that we can worship him together.

CONTENTS

PART 3: JIHAD IN JUDEO-CHRISTIAN
CONTEXT

PREFACE

A BETTER WAY FORWARD

UNTIL VERY RECENTLY, I strongly resisted writing this book. During a conversation with my editor this April, I informed him explicitly that I never wanted to write a book on jihad because the topic is so charged that even broaching the subject makes one's intentions appear suspect. This was the case even though, because of my Muslim upbringing, I receive hundreds of questions about the peacefulness of American Muslims in light of radical Islam. For the sake of keeping my message and intentions clear, I had decided to answer such questions on an individual basis rather than publishing a book on the matter.

But seven weeks ago, on November 13 of 2015, terrorists launched a coordinated assault on Paris. The West reeled in a way I had not seen since the July 7, 2005, bombings of London a decade before. Jihad had struck close to home once again, and the question of Islam's relationship with peace and violence was at the forefront of the public's mind.

The question was made exponentially more pressing by the reality of nearly 4,600,000 Syrian refugees hoping to find a haven in the West. Compassion urges us to open our doors, but prudence counters that we should think twice. How can we tell the difference between a Syrian refugee fleeing ISIS and a covert operative infiltrating the US on their behalf? While rescuing foreign innocents, might we accidentally endanger our own?

It was in the throes of this deliberation that America experienced its most deadly terrorist attack since September 11, 2001, the San Bernardino shootings on December 2, 2015. Public angst toward Islam skyrocketed to unprecedented heights, beyond even 2001 in my personal estimation. It was during this time that I began to consider the safety of my parents and relatives from potential retaliation. Even my own security crossed my mind, as frustration against radical Islam had reached a fever pitch and anyone who even looked Muslim was prone to feel suspicious eyes.

As the dust settled and it became clear that one of the shooters was an immigrant, US presidential candidate Donald Trump took a stand. He had already suggested that the government keep a database of Syrian refugees, but on December 7 he suggested an even more rigorous measure: a temporary ban on all Muslim immigration. The dilemma of discerning between radical Muslims and peaceful Muslims was cast into the spotlight once more. Many concerned Americans took a stand against Trump's suggestion, including me.

Another concerned American, a professor at Wheaton College, decided to show her solidarity with Muslims by donning a hijab and proclaiming her support for Muslims who, she said, "worship the same God" as Christians. On December 15, Wheaton placed the professor on administrative leave to consider whether her views were theologically in line with those of the university. The highly polarized public response included statements of approbation and condemnations of bigotry, and many of the voices had neither clarity nor charity.

I spent Christmas Day writing a blog response entitled "Do Muslims and Christians Worship the Same God?" an expanded version of which constitutes Question 13 in this book. The feedback I received confirmed a growing suspicion in my mind: There is too much confusion, too much misdirected anger, too much misinformation, too little balance, and too little grace to remain silent any longer.

Most responses I have seen to the present crisis are polarized, either dismissing violent jihad as irrelevant to Islam or asserting that all Muslims should be treated as potential threats. In this book, I hope to clarify both the reality of violent jihad in Islam and a compassionate approach to our Muslim neighbors.

The year 2015 ended with a *USA Today* headline, "The World Is on New Year's Eve Alert." I couldn't help but see the vague and alarming title as emblematic of the whole year. The first news report of 2016 that I read was of a mass shooting in Tel Aviv, the shooter smiling as he shot indiscriminately into a bar, his backpack containing a Quran. This year will be pivotal in American politics, and I do not doubt that polarized opinions will intensify, not least because terrorist attacks may do the same. But there are lives in the balance, and we must respond carefully. I cannot feign impartiality. Ignoring the reality of jihad endangers my nation, while responding with fear endangers my Muslim family.

There is a better way forward, a way that upholds both truth and compassion. I pray that is what you will find in the pages of this book.

ACKNOWLEDGMENTS

MANY PEOPLE worked together to produce this book at lightning speed, from conception to execution in less than three weeks. In no particular order, I would like to thank Madison Trammel and the Zondervan team for being open to my unorthodox notions of how quickly a book should be published. I would also like to thank my literary agent, Mark Sweeney, for his consistent presence and encouragement. Thanks is also due to Dr. Ravi Zacharias, Sarah Davis, and the RZIM team for their support and enthusiasm.

I must also acknowledge and thank David Cook, Sean Oliver-Dee, Richard Shumack, Daniel Brubaker, and Lincoln Loo for reading the book and providing me with their invaluable feedback. Also, almost everything I have written is in some way related to Mark Mittelberg, and I am once again indebted to him for his hand in this book.

Finally, I would like to thank my indomitable bride, Michelle, for being so patient with me as I had to be absent at the spur of the moment to fulfill this vision. I would be nowhere without you, my love.

FURTHER READING
AND INDEBTEDNESS

THIS BOOK is not intended as a comprehensive treatment of jihad, but simply as a primer that will clarify certain questions and point to a better way forward. It focuses on the historical roots of Islam more than other valid areas of exploration. Some important topics that are not covered in this book include the developments in jihad theology during the classical and colonial eras among Muslims, for example, as well as details on political motives for specific groups of radical Muslims and an exploration of Islamic eschatology.

For those who wish to learn more about jihad, including the subfields I mention above, I strongly recommend the work of David Cook, an Islamic studies professor at Rice University under whose tutelage I had the privilege of learning for a short season. Many of my thoughts about jihad have been shaped by his research, and much of what you find in this book has been distilled from his 2005 publication, *Understanding Jihad*. That book has been recently updated and addresses the subject of jihad proper with great depth and erudition, though by virtue of its scholastic precision it is perhaps less personal and less accessible than this book, which is aimed at a broader audience.

INTRODUCTION

UNDERSTANDING JIHAD AND OUR MUSLIM NEIGHBORS

SEPTEMBER 11, 2001, was an earthquake in my life, the first in a series of tectonic shifts that ultimately changed me forever.

At the time I was an eighteen-year-old American Muslim, proud of being both American and Muslim. My family had taught me to love my country, and not just by their words. My father lived this teaching by serving in the US Navy throughout my childhood, starting as a seaman and retiring as a lieutenant commander. His time serving his country, combined with the years an uncle served in the US Army and another uncle served in the US Air Force, added up to the better part of a century. Growing up, I was surrounded by Muslims who loved and served America.

But our allegiance was to God and country; we were Muslim, first and foremost. As with Americans of other religious backgrounds, our faith was in no way exclusive of our devotion to our nation. According to my parents' teaching, it was Islam that commanded me to love and serve my country. Islam taught me to defend the oppressed, to stand up for the rights of women and children, to shun the desires of the flesh, to seek the pleasure of God, and to enjoin the good and forbid the evil. By my teenage years I enthusiastically proclaimed Islam to all who would listen, and I usually started by informing them of a teaching that was knit into the fiber of my beliefs: Islam is a religion of peace.

On September 11, I was confronted for the first time with the stark reality of jihad. It was not as if I had never heard of jihad before; I certainly had, but I knew it as a defensive effort buried deep in the pages of Islamic history. That is how our imams alluded to jihad, and we never questioned it. As American Muslims we rarely, if ever, thought about jihad.

When the twin towers fell, the eyes of the nation turned to American Muslims for an explanation. I sincerely believe September 11 was a greater shock for American Muslims like my family than for the average American. Not only did we newly perceive our lack of security from jihadists, as did everyone else, we also faced a latent threat of retaliation from would-be vigilantes. It felt as if we were hemmed in on all sides. In the midst of this, while mourning our fallen compatriots and considering our own security, we had to defend the faith we knew and loved. We had to assure everyone that Islam was a religion of peace, just as we had always known. I remember hearing a slogan at my mosque that I shared with many: "The terrorists who hijacked the planes on September 11 also hijacked Islam."

Many Americans proved understanding and received our responses graciously. They joined us in denouncing terrorists, asserting that they were not representative of Islam. Others, including friends at my university, were not so compliant. They pushed back, pointing to the violence in Islamic history. Given the prevalence of warfare throughout the history of Islam, they asked how I could argue that Islam was a religion of peace.

In that defensive posture, discussing the matter with people who appeared unfriendly to my faith, it was a knee-jerk reaction for me to say whatever I could to defend Islam. But when I was alone with my thoughts, I could ask myself honestly: What does Islam really teach about jihad? Is Islam really a religion of peace?

I began to investigate the Quran and the traditions of Muhammad's life, and to my genuine surprise, I found the pages of Islamic history dripping with violence. How could I reconcile this with what I had always been taught about Islam? When I asked teachers in the Muslim community for help, they usually rationalized the violence as necessary or dismissed the historicity of the accounts. At first I followed their reasoning, but after hearing the same explanations for dozens if not hundreds of accounts, I began to realize that these were facile responses. Their explanations were similar to my own knee-jerk responses to non-Muslims who questioned Islam. Of course, I understood why they were doing it. We truly believed Islam was a religion of peace, and we were interpreting the data to fit what we knew to be true.

But was it true? After years of investigation, I had to face the reality. There is a great deal of violence in Islam, even in the very foundations of the faith, and it is not all defensive. Quite to the contrary, if the traditions about the prophet of Islam are in any way reliable, then Islam glorifies violent jihad arguably more than any other action a Muslim can take.

This conclusion led me to a three-pronged fork in the road. Either I could become an apostate and leave Islam, grow apathetic and ignore the prophet, or become "radicalized" and obey him. The alternative of simply disregarding Muhammad's teachings and continuing as a devout Muslim was not an option in my mind, nor is it for most Muslims, since to be Muslim is to submit to Allah and to follow Muhammad. Apostasy, apathy, or radicalization; those were my choices.

FROM MY STORY TO MUSLIMS TODAY

My experience of Islam is, of course, my own, but my continued interactions with hundreds of Muslims have confirmed for me that my experience as an American Muslim is not far from the norm. Perhaps my parents were more devout than most, my family more patriotic, my sect more explicitly peaceful, but by and large I see my own former thoughts and convictions in the devout American Muslims I encounter today.

In addition, the present climate in America is more than ever reminiscent of the days and months following September 11. The public at large is questioning whether Islam is a religion of peace, just like before, and I regularly encounter Muslims who are providing the same defenses and explanations that I provided after September 11.

I do not doubt, therefore, that Muslims who investigate the history of Islam from the primary sources are concluding, as I did, that the foundations of Islam are violent. Such Muslims are faced with the same choices I faced: apostasy, apathy, or radicalization. For them, radicalization is not just a paranoid hypothetical, but a potential reality.

Thousands of Muslims raised in the West have become *mujahideen*, fighters with various jihad groups, even though the battles are often centered in Middle Eastern countries. Presently, twice as many British Muslims fight for ISIS than for Britain's armed forces, leaving their peaceful Muslim families grieving. This includes young women, such as the tragic case of the three girls from Bethnal Green in London.

Countless Muslim families are shocked and bewildered at how their peaceful children or siblings become radicalized and commit mass murder. Four examples that come to mind immediately are the Boston Marathon bombers' mother, a brother of one of the *mujahideen* in the Paris massacre, the brother-in-law of the San Bernardino shooters, and the family of the shooter in Tel Aviv. Watching televised reactions of these family members has been heartwrenching.

But the families ought not be so bewildered. There is a consistent thread running through each and every example of such radicalization. The radicalized Muslims were explicitly introduced to violent traditions of early Islam, they became convinced of their authenticity, and they intentionally chose to follow them. Whether or not this is always the defining factor for radicalization should not cloud the fact that it is a universal factor. There is no need to remain bewildered when *mujahideen* themselves often tell us their reasons for becoming radicalized. If we would listen carefully to what they have to say, we would find this to be true without exception.

Of course, there is a reason why both Muslims and non-Muslims might want to avoid the elephant in the room. Acknowledging violence built into the foundations of Islam could lead people to see Islam as a necessarily violent religion, and by uncritical extension, it might lead people to see all Muslims as inherently or latently violent people. We must boldly assert that these are false and dangerous conclusions, but that does not mean we ought to close our eyes to a common impetus for radicalization. Until we diagnose and respond to the actual causes of radicalization, we will continue to lose the sons and daughters of peaceful Muslim parents to terrorism.

EIGHTEEN QUESTIONS

Just as September 11 was a pivotal juncture in my life and ultimately led me to study the primary sources of Islamic history, so this is a watershed moment for many Muslims who are presently wrestling with the path they will take. Some may very well choose jihad. If we care about these young men and women and the peaceful Muslim families that will be left distraught in the wake of their radicalization, to say nothing of the thousands of innocents whose lives they may take in the name of jihad, it is critical that we carefully and thoughtfully engage jihad with both truth and compassion. We cannot close our eyes or indulge in wishful thinking.

At the same time, we must be careful not to slide down the slippery slope of assuming every Muslim is a threat. Of the thousands of Muslims I have known in my personal life, only one has become radicalized to the point of explicitly supporting violence, and none have actually undertaken violent jihad. It is wrong to paint all Muslims with the same brush; we need to see them as individuals, the vast majority of whom just wish to live life, take care of their families, and peacefully honor God.

I do not claim to have all the answers, especially answers regarding public policy, but there is certainly a first step in responding well to radical Islam, whether individually or collectively. We must understand it for what it is. To that end, I will respond in the pages ahead to eighteen questions people most commonly ask me about jihad. These questions explore the origins of jihad, the nature of jihad today, and the phenomenon of jihad in Judeo-Christian context. After answering these questions, I will conclude by proposing a response to jihad, in my view the best way forward.

FOR THE SAKE OF CLARITY

In my response to the questions that follow, I am not suggesting that my interpretation of Islam is the only correct one, nor that those who practice Islam as a religion of peace are doing so illegitimately. My goal is more modest. I simply aim to uncover the violence that suffuses the foundations of Islam, which are the Quran and the traditions of Muhammad's life, and to demonstrate that a return to these foundations can yield violent results.

In other words, I am not arguing against the legitimacy of an Islam that moves away from its foundations, whether organically through centuries of tradition and jurisprudence or synthetically through an intentional re-envisioning of Islam by progressive Muslim thought leaders. But as long as Islam is practiced in a way that calls Muslims to return to its foundations, violence will follow.

There are certainly additional factors that can motivate Muslims towards radical Islam, whether personal factors such as a search for identity or political factors such as a response to governmental oppression. Whatever the additional factors might be, however, the foundations and history of the religion do more than simply enable the use of violence for Islamic dominance; they command it.

Nevertheless, most Muslims in the world are not violent people, despite their desire to intentionally and genuinely follow Islam. That is why I hope to also explain their perspectives, so we can understand our Muslim neighbors and show them the love and compassion that all people deserve, devoid of fear and mistrust.

Finally, it behooves me to mention that I am a Christian who left Islam after investigating the foundations of Islam and Christianity. This subject matter is deeply personal to me, and I do not pretend to be unbiased, especially since all people are biased to varying degrees. That said, in this book I am trying to be as objective as I can be in presenting the information about jihad without judgment. I try to keep explicit Christian views out of the discussion, although a few certainly come through in the eighteenth Question and in the conclusion. I ask your pardon, but I really do feel that the Christian teaching of loving one's enemies, even in the face of death, might perhaps be the most powerful answer to jihad at our disposal today. Not only does it allow us to counter jihad, it also enables us to treat Muslims with the utmost dignity: as image bearers of God.

Part 1

THE ORIGINS
OF JIHAD

WHAT IS ISLAM?

THERE ARE PRESENTLY 1.6 billion Muslims globally, making Islam the world's second largest religion, and there are probably as many answers to the question "What is Islam?" as there are adherents. The many individual expressions of the faith are valid experiences that give us insight into the lived reality of Islam. For that reason, it will be useful to start by sharing my personal experience of Islam while I was still a Muslim.

MY EXPERIENCE OF ISLAM AS AN AMERICAN MUSLIM

People often speak of religion in terms of beliefs and practices, and many introductions to Islam focus on the basic beliefs of Muslims, as represented by the Six Articles of Faith, and the mandatory practices of the Five Pillars of Islam. Yet that approach seems too distant and aloof to describe my experience as a Muslim. Islam was my identity, my culture, my worldview, my pride, even my *raison d'être*. For me, Islam was more than just a religion; it was my entire way of life.

This passionate, comprehensive embrace of Islam was not unusual in my childhood environment. My great-grandparents were Muslim missionaries to Uganda, my grandparents were

Muslim missionaries to Indonesia, my great-uncle was one of the earliest Muslim missionaries to the United States, and my uncle built one of the first mosques in the United States. While these relatives are idiosyncratic to my story, the convictions of my parents are reflective of many devout American Muslims. They were wholly dedicated to raising me as a pious Muslim child in what they perceived to be a morally permissive Western context.

What this meant in essence was a constant remembrance of Allah and the teachings of Muhammad throughout my day, from waking to sleeping. Literally. Upon waking I was taught to recite an Arabic prayer thanking Allah for giving me life; when lying down to sleep I prayed another prayer, affirming that my living and dying were in the name of Allah. Ceremonial washings and memorized prayers filled my daily routine. My parents even taught me a standard prayer to pray on every occasion for which there was no other scripted prayer.

In addition to acts of ceremonial devotion, there were dozens of legal commandments intended to protect the community and glorify Allah. Men were forbidden to wear silk or gold, women were required to maintain modesty and veil themselves accordingly, and all Muslims were prohibited from usury and interest in their monetary transactions. Some commands functioned as identity markers for our Muslim community, such as the proscription of pork and alcohol and the mandate to fast during Ramadan.

Community was, of course, incredibly important for us as minorities. The majority of Americans did not understand us and we felt it all the time, whether it be in the innocuous mispronouncing of our names or the suspicious sideward glances at my mother's and sister's burqas. The mosque served as a haven where we could gather with others who experienced life in the same way we did. Grievances from foreign lands were often laid to rest within our American Muslim community, as our local mosque was open to Sunni and Shia, Sufi and Ahmadi, Indian and Pakistani, rich and poor, black and white. Of course, my parents maintained stronger ties with those of our particular sect and heritage, but as a member of the American Muslim community we were focused on affirming Muslim unity and identity. The mosque was our outpost where we could gather as one and pursue God together.

More importantly to me than all of this, Islam taught me to lower my gaze before women, to refrain from lust and other desires of the flesh, to respond to temptation by fasting, to consider the less fortunate and oppressed, to restrain myself from anger, to always tell the truth, to honor my parents and elders, and to follow countless other virtuous morals that we often saw lacking in the amoral world around us.

Through it all, what drove us ideologically were Allah and the prophet of Islam. God, in his mercy, had sent guidance to mankind time and again, though man in his ignorance had rejected the messengers of Allah. Ultimately, Allah sent his chief messenger, Muhammad, to guide people as the perfect exemplar. Unparalleled in wisdom, character, and spiritual devotion, Muhammad led the new Muslim community from ignorance, through oppression, and into glorious victory for the sake of Allah. Since Muhammad was the perfect exemplar, we followed his practices as best we could.

That was why we lived how we lived. We were following Muhammad, our paragon and perfect prophet. Whatever Muhammad did or said, we were to aspire to the same for the sake of following and glorifying Allah. That was my experience of Islam, and it taught me to live a moral life and to pursue the pleasure of God. By and large, this is the experience of the average devout American Muslim today.

SO WHAT IS ISLAM?

But is Islam simply what Muslims experience, or is it something more? The sociologically inclined might say that Islam is simply the sum experience of all Muslims, but I would disagree, as would most Muslims. Islam is an entity beyond its people. Even if there were no one to experience it, we could still talk about Islam. Islam exists beyond experience.

In my opinion, religions ought to be defined by the identifying characteristics that distinguished the earliest community from all others. For Islam, this boils down to exclusive worship of Allah and obedience to Muhammad. This understanding is verified by the *shahada*, the proclamation that every Muslim must recite in order to become Muslim: "There is no god but Allah and Muhammad is his Messenger." Even the prophet of Islam taught that this was sufficient to make one a Muslim.

There is much more to the religion of Islam, but at its core are the teachings of Muhammad and the worship of no other god than the one he proclaimed, Allah. These teachings are contained within Muslim scripture, the Quran, and in isolated traditions of Muhammad, often referred to collectively as hadith.

DEMOGRAPHICS AND DENOMINATIONS

Yet Muslims interpret Muhammad's teachings very differently, often along partisan lines of authoritative interpreters and cultural boundaries. That is why, in very broad strokes, Shia Islam looks different from Sunni Islam, why Bosnian Islam looks different from Saudi Islam, why folk Islam in the outlands of Yemen looks different from scholarly Islam in the halls of Al-Azhar University in Cairo.

Although the core of Islam is centered on the person of Muhammad in seventh century Arabia, the expression of Islam reflects local customs. That is one reason why it is important to remember that Islam is not primarily a religion of Arabs. The country with the most Muslims in the world is Indonesia, followed by Pakistan, India, and then Bangladesh. None of those nations are Arab, and local customs manage to find their way into Islamic expression.

In addition, no two Muslims are exactly alike, and that is another reason why the expression of Islam is so varied. My sister and I were raised in the same sect (see appendix D) by the same parents, but her practice and interpretation of Islam looks very different from how mine looked. Her leanings were far more Western and pluralist than were mine. I was more interested in learning about Muhammad and his teachings than she was, while she was more interested in American pop culture than I was.

MUSLIMS ARE NOT ISLAM

Especially because of the great diversity of Islamic expression, it bears repeating that Islam is not Muslims, and Muslims are not Islam. Though Muslims are adherents of Islam, and Islam is the worldview of Muslims, the two are not the same, as many uncritically believe.

On one end of the spectrum, many assume that if the Quran teaches something then all Muslims believe it. That is false. Many Muslims have not heard of a given teaching, some might interpret it differently, and others may frankly do their best to ignore it. For example, even if we were to demonstrate through careful hermeneutics that the Quranic injunction to beat disobedient wives (4:34) is meant to apply to all Muslims today, it would still have zero bearing in my family. My father would never beat my mother.

On the other end of the spectrum, criticism of Islam is often taken to be criticism of Muslims. That is equally false. One can criticize the Quranic command to beat disobedient wives without criticizing Muslims. The accusation of Islamophobia, discussed in Question 12, often fails at this point. Islam is not Muslims, and one can criticize Islam while affirming and loving Muslims.

CONCLUSION

Thus Islam is defined by obedience to Muhammad's teachings and worship of no other god but the one he proclaimed, Allah. Although there are as many as 1.6 billion expressions of Islam in the world, Muslims are not themselves Islam. In my experience as an American Muslim, there was absolutely no emphasis placed on violence, but a great deal of emphasis placed on morality, legality, community, and spirituality. For me and all the American Muslims I knew, Islam was a religion of peace with God and peace with man.

But my experience of Islam is not the only one, and it cannot define Islam. For other Muslims, violence is a part of their expression of Islam, but their experience is no more definitive than mine was.

To answer whether Islam truly is a religion of peace, we must consider what Islam teaches, not just what Muslims practice.

IS ISLAM "A RELIGION OF PEACE"?

SINCE I WAS BORN, I was taught by imams and my family that Islam is "a religion of peace." What is surprising, in retrospect, is that this popular slogan may not have been around much earlier than that.

THE MEANING OF THE WORD *ISLAM*

Mark Durie, a research scholar of linguistics and Islam at Melbourne School of Theology, informs us in an article for the *Independent Journal*, "Islam was first called 'the religion of peace' as late as 1930, in the title of a book published in India. . . . The phrase was slow to take off, but by the 1970s it was appearing more and more frequently in the writings of Muslims for western audiences."

Whether or not one agrees that the slogan first appeared in the twentieth century, it is beyond dispute that the Quran never says, "Islam is the religion of peace," nor do the traditions of Muhammad.

This common misconception may stem from another, the oft-repeated assertion that *Islam* means "peace." It does not. The Arabic word *Islam* means "surrender," though it is related to the word for peace, *salaam*. Durie sheds light on the nature of the relationship and the origin of the word *Islam*: "The word Islam is based upon a military metaphor. Derived from *aslama*, 'surrender,' its primary meaning is to make oneself safe (*salama*) through surrender. In its original meaning, a Muslim was someone who surrendered in warfare."

In our Islamic community, we were taught that the "surrender" of Islam was a submission of one's will and life to God, which I would argue is noble and does not connote violence. But to contend that the word *Islam* signifies peace in the absence of violence is incorrect. *Islam* signifies a peace after violence, or under the threat of it.

According to Islamic tradition, that is how Muhammad himself used the word. His warning to neighboring tribes is famous: *Aslim taslam*, "If you surrender, you will have peace." It was a play on words, as *aslim* also connotes becoming Muslim: "If you convert, you will have safety through surrender."

So the word *Islam* refers to the peace that comes from surrender. Peaceful Muslim communities today present that imagery as a spiritual peace with Allah, but records of Muhammad's life indicate that the notion of submission was also used in military contexts.

FROM ETYMOLOGY TO HISTORY

A more appropriate avenue for answering whether Islam is "a religion of peace" is the life and teachings of its prophet. The Quran and the traditions of Islam's prophet are far more definitive than the etymology of the word *Islam*.

I will discuss this further in Question 4, but suffice it to say for now that no one can honestly deny the presence of violence in both the Quran and the life of the prophet of Islam. From the time Muhammad first obtained a following that could successfully fight, he launched raids and battles every year until he died. According to David Cook in *Understanding Jihad*, he commissioned or personally participated in eighty-six battles during that time, which is more than nine battles a year. The Quran refers often to these campaigns, many times in approbation. For example, chapter 8 of the Quran is about the Muslims' first major battle, the battle of Badr, and it teaches that Allah is the one who led the Muslims, that he compelled the Muslims to attack the Meccans, that he supplied them with angelic assistance, and that he was the one who slew the Meccans through the hands of the Muslims. There is no avoiding the presence and even glorification of violence in this chapter or elsewhere throughout Islam's origins.

The battles of the early Muslim community seem to have escalated in a crescendo toward the end of Muhammad's life, not halting with his death but rather catapulting into global proportions. As soon as the prophet of Islam died, there came the apostate wars, then the overthrow of Persia, and then the campaigns of Egypt and beyond. Within two centuries of the advent of Islam, Muslim conquests expanded Islamic territory from the shores of the Atlantic well into the valleys of India. At the end of that era, the most influential hadith collectors gathered whole books documenting Muhammad's conduct and commands during times of warfare. Shortly after them, the great Islamic jurists systematically codified *sharia*, Islamic law, devoting whole branches of jurisprudence to the proper practice of warfare.

For these reasons, no one can claim that "Islam is a religion of peace" in the sense that the religion has been historically devoid of violence, neither in its origins nor in the history of the global Muslim community. Apart from the first thirteen years of Islamic history, when there were not enough Muslims to fight, Islam has always had an elaborate practice or doctrine of war.

IN WHAT WAY MIGHT ISLAM BE A RELIGION OF PEACE?

In my experience, most Muslims who repeat this slogan have not critically considered the history of Islam. Those who have and continue to say it mean it in one of two senses: a spiritual sense or an idealized sense. In the spiritual sense it is understood that Islam brings peace to a person through personal discipline, a right relationship with other Muslims, and submission toward the Creator. This sense of the slogan is irrelevant as a response to violent jihad.

In the idealized sense, it is generally meant that Islam brings peace to this world. Though battles have been fought, they were fought out of necessity. Ideally, the goal that Islam strives for is peace throughout the world. According to this sense, Islam can be a religion of peace despite the presence of war, so this sense of the slogan is also irrelevant as a response to violent jihad. (Some who espouse this view argue that the wars in the foundation of Islam were defensive endeavors, an argument that I will consider in Question 4.)

THE WEST AND THE RELIGION OF PEACE

Unfortunately, neither of these more viable and nuanced approaches appears to be in mind when Western media and Western leaders proclaim that Islam is a religion of peace. Rather, such proclamations appear to be little more than attempts to change public perception of Islam, albeit for a noble cause such as precluding retaliation against innocent Muslims. We often hear the loudest proclamations of Islam's peacefulness in the wake of the most heinous jihadist violence. President George W. Bush called Islam peaceful after September 11, Prime Minister Tony Blair after the July 7 London bombings, and President François Hollande after the Charlie Hebdo massacre. This regular juxtaposition of extreme Islamist violence with a strong insistence that Islam is a religion of peace is obviously jarring, and not just to Westerners.

The Syrian Sheikh Ramadan al-Buti, considered one of the most influential traditionalist Sunni scholars in the world, saw an insistence on Islam's peacefulness as an effort by the West to emasculate Islam. If Western leaders and Western media repeat it enough, perhaps Muslims will begin to believe it. He asserted in *The Jurisprudence of the Prophetic Biography* that the West was seeking to "erase the notion of jihad from the minds of all Muslims." In asserting this position, the sheikh showed characteristic Middle Eastern candor in his assessment of peace and violence in Islam. Tragically, he was himself killed by a suicide bomber in 2013.

CONCLUSION

Instead of seeking to redefine Islam, we should consider more thoughtful and honest approaches. The question of whether Islam can be a religion of peace in spiritual or idealized senses ought to be considered, but the implication that Islam is a religion devoid of violence is simply false. The frequent proclamations by leaders and media members of Islam's peacefulness may be intended well, but more is needed than good intentions.

Instead, we must open our eyes and not allow ourselves to remain blind to evident facts in our attempts to either protect or sway Muslims. Though violence is writ large throughout the pages of Islamic history, including in its foundations, that does not mean our Muslim neighbors are violent. Muslims deserve to be treated with the kindness and respect due to all people.

In fact, their journeys may be leading many of them to confront Islam's violence for the first time, as my journey once did, and they, too, may be approaching a critical three-pronged fork in the road. May our eyes and our arms both be open to them.

WHAT IS JIHAD?

THE *ENCYCLOPEDIA OF ISLAM* defines jihad in this way: "In law, according to general doctrine and in historical tradition, the *djihad* consists of military action with the object of the expansion of Islam and, if need be, of its defence." This is a fairly standard definition of jihad among scholars of Islam in the West.

In broader Muslim literature there appears to be no such widely accepted definition, but that makes sense given the various kinds of jihad and the myriad applications of the term found in classical and modern Islamic literature. The primary meaning of jihad as used by pre-modern Muslim jurists is "warfare with spiritual significance." This definition appeals more to me than the standard scholarly definition, because it reflects the reality of a less than rigid use of the term.

The popular definition of jihad as "Islamic holy war" is misleading. The words *holy war* are charged with connotations of the Christian Crusades, but the impetus and theological justification of the crusades were markedly different from jihad, as I will explore in Question 17.

THE DEVELOPING DOCTRINE OF JIHAD

Part of the reason why jihad is so difficult to define is that the Arabic word itself means "strife" or "struggle," and it is not always used in a doctrinal sense. The Quran appears to use the term to mean a "struggle for spiritual purposes," at times remaining ambiguous about whether a violent or non-violent struggle is in view. In fact, some verses do use the word *jihad* as a purely spiritual struggle, such as 22:78.

That said, the Quran frequently uses the word in reference to a violent struggle for spiritual purposes. A clear example of this is a discussion of warfare in 2:216–18 which culminates in Allah's approval of those who undertake this jihad: "Warfare is prescribed for you, though you dislike it. . . . Behold, those who believe, emigrate, and undertake jihad, these have hope of the mercy of Allah." It is incorrect to argue, as do some apologists for Islam in the West, that the word can only refer to a spiritual struggle. Even in the Quran that is demonstrably false, let alone in the traditions of Muhammad's life.

In fact, when it comes to the hadith, far and away the most frequent context of jihad is violent physical struggle. I will explore this further in Question 4, but for now I want to merely note that this meaning makes sense when we consider the time during which the canonical hadith collections were compiled, which was at the pinnacle of Islamic conquests. The Muslim community then preserved those traditions that were most relevant to them. In so doing, they solidified the term *jihad* in the direction of a violent spiritual struggle.

By the time of the great Muslim jurists, the generations that founded various schools of Islamic thought and enumerated codes of *sharia*, jihad had developed into a fairly systematized doctrine of warfare. Conditions and rules of jihad conduct had been developed based on the relevant verses of the Quran and hadith traditions of Muhammad.

For example, jihad could not be the endeavor of a rogue Muslim, but had to be formally declared by a legitimate authority among the Muslim people, most likely the caliph, the leader of the Muslims (see appendix C). The impetus for jihad must be of critical importance for the religion of Islam itself, or at least for a great number of Muslims. The causes ought to be specified prior to engaging in warfare, as well as the terms for resolution. These rules of conduct explain why al-Qaida regularly broadcasted proclamations of jihad with Osama bin Laden prominently displayed as an authority, airing lists of grievances against the West and demands for the cessation of hostilities. The endeavor was not simply for dramatic purposes, but also to fulfill the classical conditions for appropriately launching jihad.

There are other requirements of jihad that classical jurists upheld, conditions that were grounded in Muhammad's teachings for the sake of humane warfare. These included refraining from killing non-combatants or looting their property, restraint from disfiguring the corpses of fallen enemies, prohibitions against scorched-earth policies, and more. Depending on the jurist, treatments of jihad differed in exact rules and emphases. Although many jurists appeared concerned with combatant conduct for legalistic purposes, by the classical era of Islam there was a definite concern for moral warfare and attempts to limit collateral damage by some jurists.

Of course, the mere enumeration of rules of jihad did not necessitate their enforcement, and it is clear that Muslims did not always follow them. For example, non-combatants were frequently slaughtered in eighth- and ninth-century Islamic conquests. In addition, Muslim-on-Muslim jihad was proclaimed at times during the classical era, even though these pronouncements should have been categorized as non-jihad hostilities. To be clear, examples of Muslim-on-Muslim violence in the past were not the same as contemporary Muslim-on-Muslim jihad, which is often rationalized by accusing enemies of being apostates. This is a modern development, though with ancient roots, as I will demonstrate in Question 7.

Although the concept of jihad continues to develop to this

day, one theme remains consistent. Because jihad is a struggle for spiritual purposes, a *mujahid* enjoys the benefit of Allah's blessing. This promise is in the Quran itself, and it partially explains the prevalence of jihad throughout Islamic history, especially among those most zealous for Allah's approval.

THE USE OF TERROR

Although the Quran probably does not envision something similar to twenty-first century terrorism, it does command Muslims to use terror and spread fear: "Prepare against them all the strength and war horses that you can to strike terror into the enemies of Allah and your enemies."

This teaching of the Quran is corroborated through the hadith, as Muhammad said, "I have been made victorious with terror" (Sahih al-Bukhari 4.52.220). Casting fear into the heart of Allah's enemies is thus enjoined in the Quran and has a precedent in Muhammad's life.

THE GREATER JIHAD AND THE LESSER JIHAD

A regular feature in Western scholarly discussions about jihad is the distinction between the greater jihad and the lesser jihad. The account reads: "A number of fighters came to the Messenger of Allah, and he said: 'You have done well in coming from the lesser jihad to the greater jihad.' They said: 'What is the greater jihad?' He said: 'For the servant [of God] to fight his passions'" (Al-Bayhaqi, *Al-Zuhd al-Kabir*). From this tradition, a number of scholars and apologists defend the notion that jihad ought to be primarily understood as a spiritual struggle and secondarily understood as a physical one.

Although Sufi Muslims did develop the notion of "greater jihad" beginning in the twelfth century, there are significant problems with using the quotation above as a proof text for the primacy of peaceful jihad. Perhaps the most significant problem is that the Quran teaches the exact opposite. In 4:95, the Quran says, "Not equal are those believers who are sedentary, other than the disabled, and those who undertake jihad in the cause of Allah with their wealth and their lives. Allah has granted a grade higher to those who strive with their wealth and lives than to those who sit." The exemption for the disabled makes the verse particularly clear. Physical fighting is more virtuous than not, according to the Quran.

This may be why none of the canonical collections of hadith include the tradition of the greater jihad; those compilers either did not know the hadith or considered it too dubious for inclusion in their collections.

As Muslim scholars assert, and as Western scholars ought to agree, it is inappropriate to look at an entire doctrine through the lens of a single hadith, especially if that tradition is not in any of the canonical collections. The fact that the tradition directly contravenes a Quranic teaching should put the matter out of dispute: The notion that spiritual jihad is greater than physical jihad has no place in the foundations of Islam.

THE "SIXTH PILLAR" OF ISLAM

On the contrary, physical jihad was given such a place of prominence in the foundations of Islam that it has been honorifically referred to by some Muslim scholars as "the sixth pillar." The Five Pillars of Islam are the minimum practices incumbent on all Muslims: proclaiming the *shahada*, reciting daily prayers, paying alms, fasting during Ramadan, and performing the pilgrimage to Mecca. However, in the canonical hadith collections, a great emphasis is also placed on the Muslim's duty to participate in jihad. Perhaps this is why, even in the earliest categorized hadith collections, the sections on jihad usually followed immediately after the sections on the Five Pillars. These traditions, as we shall see ahead, seem to imply that fighting is a requisite duty of all who are able.

CONCLUSION

Though the word *jihad* literally means "struggle," and the Quran at times uses it in a spiritual context, the primary use of the word has always implied a physical struggle for spiritual purposes. The doctrine of jihad has been developing from the time of the Quran until today, in the classical era being expounded to include a code of conduct with injunctions designed to preserve innocent lives and lessen collateral damage. These rules, however, have not always been enforced.

The portrayal of jihad as primarily a spiritual endeavor, often by referring to the tradition of the "greater jihad," is inconsistent with the Quran, the canonical hadith collections, Islamic history, and classical Islamic hermeneutics. It is an argument that has little grounding in reality. On the contrary, the foundations of Islam consistently portray jihad as primarily a physical struggle, as we will now explore.

IS JIHAD IN THE QURAN AND THE LIFE OF MUHAMMAD?

IT IS HELPFUL to provide some context about the average Muslim's encounter with the Quran and hadith before diving into this question. Even though the Quran and the hadith are the foundations of Islam, Muslims do not usually engage in systematically studying their teachings. This is true even of those Muslims who have memorized the entire Quran; though they may have memorized the Arabic recitation of the text, they often do not know how to exegete its meaning.

This begins to make more sense when we remember that most Muslims are not Arabs, and they do not natively speak Arabic. In fact, nobody natively speaks the Arabic of the Quran, as classical Arabic has given way to colloquial forms of Arabic that differ significantly throughout the Arab world, and the only people who speak a form of Arabic that approximates the Quran are those who have studied it in schools.

It is for this reason that, even though I had recited the entire Quran in Arabic by the age of five and memorized the last fifteen chapters by my teen years, my understanding of the Quran was limited to what I had been taught by the elders in my community.

Similarly, though I had memorized the Arabic of shorter hadith traditions, I never even touched the canonical collections of hadith. The hadith I knew were those that had been selected by my elders. Often, during Friday sermons, weekend religious classes, or the like, hadith were recounted without any reference whatsoever. I do not doubt now that some of them were probably fabricated, but I also do not doubt the good intentions of our teachers.

None of this is to point the finger at Muslims, because only a small percentage of people in any religious community endeavor to critically engage their canonical texts. The time, education, and financial resources required for such efforts are luxuries not afforded to many.

Yet the net effect of all this is that the vast majority of Muslims inherit their understanding of Islam and have not investigated the foundations of Islam for themselves. If they were raised in the West and taught that Islam is a religion of peace, as I was, then their first foray into the foundations might be somewhat of a shock, and they will probably soon find themselves either in a defensive position or grappling with significant cognitive dissonance.

MUHAMMAD'S LIFE AND ITS REFLECTION IN THE QURAN

Let's first consider the life of Muhammad as recounted in Islamic tradition and as reflected in the Quran, with a focus on peace and violence. Although there are many intractable problems that arise when studying Muhammad's life, including questions about the historical reliability of the sources, discrepant archaeological findings, the ages of Quranic manuscripts, inconsistencies in geographic reports, foreign accounts of early Islam, and problematic merchant records, none of these detract from my present aim which is to simply understand Muhammad according to Muslim tradition.

Muhammad was born in 570 AD and experienced a very

difficult childhood. His father died before he was born, his mother died shortly thereafter, and then his next caretaker, his grandfather, also died. In his young adulthood he became a merchant and was known for his integrity, wisdom, and skill.

At the age of forty, Muhammad received his call to become the prophet of Islam while meditating in a cave near Mecca. It came in the form of a revelation given to him by the angel Gabriel. These revelations were ultimately called *Quran,* and they gradually increased in frequency. His first thirteen years as the prophet of Islam were spent proclaiming these Quranic revelations to the polytheists of Mecca, primarily proclamations of monotheism. The mercantile economy of Mecca was bolstered by the pilgrimage of other polytheists to their city, which was home to 360 idols, so the polytheists of Mecca did not take kindly to Muhammad's insistence that there was only one God.

During that time, Quranic proclamations also focused on welfare for orphans and widows and fellowship with other monotheists, such as Jews and Christians. Over the course of some years, many of the humble and weak became Muslims despite the threat of persecution. Some Muslims were indeed persecuted, and a few were even martyred before Muhammad escaped Mecca on the night of an assassination attempt.

These early years of Muhammad's ministry are known as his Meccan years, and they are the only years Muhammad did not deputize or personally engage in raids or battles. The Quran reflects this era of teaching in the Meccan *suras,* or chapters, though the Quran is not neatly categorized. Meccan passages and later passages, usually referred to as "Medinan," are frequently found side by side in the same suras.

The next ten years were the last of Muhammad's life. These were his emblematic years, often called the *maghazi* years by classical Muslim commentators. *Maghazi* means "raids," and it is an appropriate description. At the end of his first year in Medina, Muhammad started launching raids and continued launching skirmishes or battles until he died. The first six such raids, however, were failures.

The first successful raid that Muhammad ordered, the Nakhla raid, was controversial and remains so 1,400 years later. On Muhammad's orders, raiders were sent to intercept a Meccan caravan quite some distance from the Muslim base of Medina. Whether by Muhammad's intention or not, the interception occurred during a holy month, a time of truce between all Arabs. The Muslim raiders shaved their heads, making it appear that they were on a pilgrimage. Upon seeing that the Muslims were observing the holy month, the Meccans let down their guard and began setting up camp. That is when the Muslims attacked, killing and capturing undefended Meccans during a sacred time of truce, a great sin in the eyes of most Arabs.

When news of this treacherous act reached Medina, even many Muslims were understandably indignant. But then came a revelation from the Quran, defending Muhammad's raiders against the inquiries of the dismayed: "They ask you about fighting in the holy months. Tell them, 'Fighting in the holy months is a great sin, but a greater sin is to prevent mankind from following the way of Allah, to disbelieve in him'. . . . [O]ppression is worse than slaughter" (2:217). According to the Quran, the Meccan oppression of keeping people from Islam was worse than slaughtering them during a time of truce. This attack by the Muslims during the holy month, not at all defensive but entirely offensive, was vindicated by the Quran.

Until this time, Muslims had only been victims, but now Allah was blessing their efforts with spoils. Understandably, Muhammad commissioned many more raids, and one of them inadvertently launched the first major battle in Islamic history. As Muhammad ordered a raid against a passing Meccan caravan, the caravan commander perceived his danger and sent to Mecca for reinforcements. The battle of Badr was the result, and the odds were against the Muslims. Despite the odds, the Muslims won the battle, and this victory has been forever etched in the spirit of Muslims because it is memorialized in the Quran.

As mentioned previously, the Quran discusses the battle in its eighth surah, the chapter of the "spoils of war." 8:42–43 describes the scene of the battle and that Muhammad had brought the Muslims to attack a caravan based on a dream that it would be lightly defended. Upon arriving, they found a large Meccan army defending the caravan, and they fought an unexpected battle. 8:7 describes the Muslims, upon seeing the Meccan army guarding the caravan, desiring to fight the lesser of the two forces, but Allah intended them to fight the stronger for the sake of "the truth." This truth, of course, is that Allah is with the Muslims who struggle for him. The Muslims gained the upper hand and killed the Meccans, though it was not the Muslims who killed, but it was Allah who killed (8:17). The chapter ends by extolling those who emigrated from Mecca and carried out jihad against the Meccans (8:72–75).

On account of this victory, the Muslims were emboldened to fight even more, and the Quran explicitly told them to be so emboldened: "O Prophet, rouse the believers to fight. If there are twenty patient men among you, they will overcome two hundred. And if there are one hundred with you, they will overcome a thousand disbelievers because they are a people who do not understand" (8:65).

Muslims increased the scope of their battles from raids to larger campaigns. In addition to raids against the Bedouins, Muslims attacked agricultural Jewish tribes to secure their fertile lands, including the Jews of Khybar, who, much like the Meccans during the Nakhla raid, were unarmed and unaware when the Muslims attacked. Muslims also fought campaigns for dominance over the Hijaz, a western region of Saudi Arabia. After Badr came the battles of Uhud, Khandaq, Mecca, and Hunain. In addition to these battles for land, Muhammad led Muslims on attacks against the Christian Byzantines at al-Muta and Tabuk, the former battle a result of Muhammad's demand that the Emperor submit to Islam, the latter a battle for plunder.

THE MIXED NATURE OF QURANIC VERSES

Most of these battles were offensive campaigns against mutual enemies. Such battles at times resulted in the complete decimation of the Muslims' enemies, such as the defeat of the Jews at Khybar, who as a result had to pay half of their agricultural produce every year as a *jizya*, or ransom tax, before being expelled from the land regardless.

Some of the battles were defensive, such as the battle of Khandaq, which was a Meccan siege of Medina. That particular battle involved new strategies of fighting, including digging trenches, that resulted in the Meccans leaving Medina after a bitter stalemate. Muhammad recouped some of his losses by decimating a tribe of Medinan Jews whom he accused of supporting the Meccans. He executed all pubescent boys and adult men, took their women and children for slaves, and divided their possessions among the Muslims, including lands the Jews owned that Muhammad had not been to before. This is recorded very briefly in the Quran (33:25–27) but with much more detail in the traditions.

Some battles were complete losses, such as the battle of Uhud wherein Muhammad was struck down and feared dead for a time. Other battles, though not as bitter, were fruitless, such as the ill-fated battle of Tabuk where the Muslims were unable to even find their enemies.

But the victory that is sweetest among all the eighty-six battles that Muhammad launched was the conquering of Mecca. Almost a decade after fleeing for his life and fighting repeatedly against the Meccans, Muhammad returned triumphantly with 10,000 warriors and conquered his homeland. What is most notable about this account is that even though these were the Muslims' most inveterate enemies, great mercy was extended as most people who did not fight the Muslim conquerors were allowed to live. Only a handful of those who surrendered were executed.

The greatly varied experiences of the early Muslims are reflected in the Quran, and not in chronological order. Therefore we can find verses commanding great peace and great violence interspersed throughout the text. There are verses that prohibit Muslims from fighting, verses that allow Muslims to fight defensively, and verses that command Muslims to fight even when they don't want to. There are verses that designate Jews and Christians as friends of Muslims and verses that call them the worst of creatures. There are verses that tell Muslims to desist from fighting those who are peaceful, and verses that command Muslims to fight those with whom they have treaties; verses that say all who believe in God and do good works will receive his mercy, and verses that say anyone who follows a religion other than Islam will not be saved. There are verses that say Allah will certainly grant victory to Muslims if they fight, and verses that say Allah was testing Muslims by allowing them to be defeated.

This is why, according to basic principles of Islamic hermeneutics, it is problematic to single out verses of the Quran and draw conclusions without considering the historical context. Since the Quranic text is not presented in chronological order, this endeavor is made more difficult. Especially when it comes to jihad, polemics are plentiful, but we ought to carefully consider assertions in light of the complex reality of Islamic traditions.

THE VIOLENT CULMINATION OF THE FOUNDATIONS OF ISLAM

Through the chronology of Muhammad's life and the Quran, there is one clear trend: The proclivity toward violence in the early Muslim community continued to increase from the moment they could fight, through Muhammad's death, and beyond. Muhammad's leadership began peacefully for thirteen years, then ventured into small raids involving only tens of fighters, then engaged in significant battles with hundreds of fighters, and finally Muhammad conquered Mecca with 10,000 soldiers and secured the lands of the Hijaz with 30,000 soldiers. By the time of his death, Muhammad had conquered the Arabian

Peninsula and most likely succeeded in his goal of cleansing it of all non-Muslims.

An increasing proclivity towards warfare is reflected in the Quran itself. The oft-cited peaceful passages, such as 2.256 and surah 109, are among the earliest passages of the Quran. After them chronologically come statements such as 2.216, which says, "You are required to fight, even if it is hard for you." Dozens, if not hundreds, of verses that suggest or command violence can be brought forth from the Quran, but the example of one particular surah will suffice.

Surah 9 of the Quran, called "the Disavowal," is the last major chapter of the Quran to be revealed, according to Islamic tradition, and it is by far the most violent chapter. Because of its sweeping commands and finality, classical Muslim theologians understood it to function as the final orders from Allah to Muhammad, nullifying the earlier, peaceful passages of the Quran. (Such nullification of former Quran passages is normative and called *abrogation*, as I will discuss in Question 5.)

The chapter begins with a disavowal. Now that the Muslims had conquered Mecca, all treaties they had made with polytheists were to be nullified, though time would be allowed for polytheists to decide whether they would convert to Islam, leave Arabia, or fight the Muslims. At the end of those months, the Muslims were commanded to "kill the polytheists wherever you find them, lay siege to them, take them captive and sit in ambush for them everywhere. If they (convert to Islam) leave their way" (9:5).

Of course, some of these polytheists were family members of recent converts to Islam. 9:23 says to the Muslims, "O believers, do not take your fathers and your brothers as family if they prefer disbelief over faith. Those of you who have friendship with them are doing wrong." This was to be the categorical end of all relationships, the disavowal, between Muslims and polytheists.

The problem with this was that polytheists who came to Mecca brought trade to the city and income to Meccan Muslims. The next section of the Quran answers those who fear the economic repercussions of killing the polytheists of Arabia: "O you who believe, surely the polytheists are impure, so do not allow them to approach the sacred mosque after this time. If you fear poverty, Allah will provide for you from His grace, if He wills" (9:28).

How exactly will Allah provide? The next verse explains: "Fight those who do not believe [in Islam] . . . from among the people of the book [the Jews and Christians] until they pay the *jizya* and feel their subjugation" (9:29). In other words, Jews and Christians will be made to pay a ransom tax, helping to ameliorate the financial loss of expelling the polytheists.

A justification must be provided for unprovoked attacks on Jews and Christians, so the next verse (9:30) provides the reasoning. "The Jews say 'Ezra is the Son of God' and the Christians say 'Christ is the Son of God.' These are the very words of their mouths, they imitate what disbelievers said before them. May Allah destroy them!" It is not the actions of the Jews and Christians but their beliefs that have earned them their doom.

The following verses continue to make it clear that Jews and Christians, according to their beliefs, have set up partners with Allah, the unforgivable sin of "shirk" in Islam, and they will receive their just punishment. "They have made their rabbis and their monks into gods other than Allah" (9:31). This makes Jews and Christians like the polytheists, and thus Muslims ought to conquer them. According to 9:33, "He [Allah] is the one who sent the messenger [Muhammad] with the guidance [Quran] and the true religion [Islam] in order to prevail over every faith." Note these last words. Islam is now to be dominant over every other faith. For this reason, Jews and Christians will be subjugated and made to pay tribute. Verses 34–35 clarify that these proclamations are still ultimately related to the financial concerns of Muslims, because they point out that the Jewish and Christian leaders have great wealth. These verses also taunt Christians, saying their "good news" is actually that they are going to hell.

So chapter 9 expands the scope of Islamic warfare tremendously. It begins as a command to disavow all treaties with poly-theists and to kill them wherever they may be found unless they convert. It continues by telling Muslims not to worry about the financial impact of this policy, as Jews and Christians deserve to be conquered for being like polytheists themselves. Out of their great wealth they ought to pay Muslims, as Islam is the best religion and will "prevail over every faith." This is the command of the last major chapter of the Quran, the final marching orders of Muhammad to his men.

JIHAD AND THE NEW BARGAIN WITH MUSLIMS

Within this chapter, we see that an incredibly expansive scope of war is the new norm for jihad.

In 9:38–39, the Quran warns Muslims that if they do not fight they will be punished. "O you who believe, what is wrong with you? . . . Have you become happy with the worldly life instead of the afterlife? . . . If you do not march forth, He will punish you with a great punishment. . . ." They are then literally commanded to fight in jihad. "March, whether heavy or light, and carry out jihad with your wealth and your lives in the way of Allah. That is good for you, if you only knew" (9:41).

Turning to Muhammad, the Quran tells him that no true Muslim would avoid jihad. "Those who believe in Allah and in the last day do not ask you to excuse them from jihad" (9:44). 9:49 goes even farther, saying that such people are already encir-cled by hell.

The words of the Quran here are important to grasp. A Muslim's willingness to engage in jihad is an indicator of whether he or she really believes in Islam. This is because the outcomes of jihad are only good. Either one receives spoils, which are good, or one receives martyrdom, which secures eternal bliss (9:52). Those who do not engage in jihad are revealed to be hypocrites. Hypocrites are a category of people often discussed in the Quran, which portrays them as people who outwardly display belief in Islam but are actually liars. It is an important category I will return to in Question 7.

As for those who do fight, 9:111 is axiomatic and essential for understanding the future developments of jihad. "Surely Allah has bought from the believers their lives and their properties in order that paradise be theirs. They fight in the way of Allah, so they kill and are killed, on which there is a true promise . . . Rejoice in the bargain you have made!" Those who fight and die in the way of Allah have made a bargain. If they die, they are guaranteed paradise. A true Muslim ought to rejoice at this, according to the Quran.

This is the salvific contract that paved the way for the zeal of early Muslim conquests. On account of this verse, later Muslims would say that "the sword wipes away sins" (Ibn Mubarak, *Kitab al-Jihad*). It is no wonder that early Muslim warriors famously said they desired death more than their enemies desired life. They believed the promise of the Quran.

The final major chapter of the Quran launched Muslims into warfare with no clear endpoint and a desire to fight to the death. This was the ethos that led to Muslims conquering fully one-third of the known world within 150 years of the advent of Islam.

OFFENSIVE VERSUS DEFENSIVE JIHAD

While many Muslims are aware of the battles in Muhammad's life, they often believe the battles were all defensive. As we have seen, that is not true, not even of the very first battles that Muslims fought. Both Nakhla and Badr were offensive endeavors. The Quran attests of Badr that Muhammad led Muslims out to battle expecting to find a lightly guarded caravan. After Muhammad had fled Mecca and had the ability to leave peacefully, it was his command that led to the first blood spilled.

The Quran in 9:29 also gives Muslims the command to fight Jews and Christians because of their beliefs, not because of any aggression on their part. This understanding is verified by

Muhammad's launching of his fighters against the Byzantines at the Battle of Tabuk, though the Byzantine Christians had never even threatened Muslims.

When I first discovered these facts, my response was to try and find a way to say they were, despite appearances, defensive battles. The raids I dismissed as historically uncertain, the battle of Badr an attempt to reclaim what Meccans had stolen, the battle of Tabuk a preemptive strike under threat of Roman attack. But these were my knee-jerk responses to defend the teachings I had inherited, and they were implausible at best. When considering the big picture, such explanations are wholly indefensible.

The early Muslim community certainly had nothing against offensive attacks, as its conquests demonstrate. Common sense precludes us from believing that the vast conquests of the early Muslims all came from defensive campaigns, but the records of the conquered remove all doubt. One such record, *The Chronicles of John, Bishop of Nikiu*, reveals what happened during the Muslim conquests of northern Egypt in 640 AD. One of Muhammad's companions, Amr ibn al-As, came with his army to an undefended city whose soldiers had run away in fear.

> Amr and the Muslim army . . . made their entry into Nakius [Nikiu] and took possession. Finding no soldiers, they proceeded to put to the sword all whom they found in the streets and in the churches, men, women, and infants. They showed mercy to none. After they had captured this city, they marched against other localities and sacked them and put all they found to the sword. . . . Let us now cease, for it is impossible to recount the iniquities perpetrated by the Muslims after their capture of the island of Nakius.

This is how history recounts one of Muhammad's companions enacting jihad. Even though the record contains the slaughter of non-combatants, it appears to be more consistent with a plain reading of surah 9 than do views of peaceful or defensive jihad.

THE HADITH AND JIHAD

What ultimately convinced me that jihad was primarily violent and often offensive was reading the hadith collections for myself. For example, in Sahih Bukhari, the collection of hadith that Sunni Muslims consider most trustworthy, we find an entire book dedicated to Muhammad's teachings on jihad. There I found a tradition in which Muhammad says, "I have been ordered to fight against the people until they testify that none has the right to be worshipped but Allah and that Muhammad is Allah's Messenger. . . . [O]nly then will they save their lives and property from me" (Sahih Bukhari 1.2.25).

Similarly in the next most reliable collection of hadith, Sahih Muslim, there is also a book on jihad, and in it Muhammad says, "I will expel the Jews and Christians from the Arabian Peninsula and will not leave any but Muslims" (Sahih Muslim 1767a).

These traditions in hadith collections that Muslims consider most authentic seem to go even further than surah 9 of the Quran. They imply that Jews and Christians will not be allowed to live in Arabia. While surah 9 does not command this of Muslims, it does not prohibit it either.

Consider another hadith that says fighting in jihad is better than praying and fasting ceaselessly.

> A man came to Allah's Messenger and said, "Instruct me as to such a deed as equals Jihad [in reward]." He replied, "I do not find such a deed." Then he added, "Can you, while the Muslim fighter is in the battle-field, enter your mosque to perform prayers without cease and fast and never break your fast?" The man said, "But who can do that?" Abu-Huraira added, "The Mujahid [Muslim fighter] is rewarded even for the footsteps of his horse while it wanders about tied in a long rope." (Sahih al-Bukhari 4.52.44)

Another hadith from the same book bolsters our understanding of surah 9, focusing on the good outcomes of jihad and Allah's bargain with Muslims.

I heard Allah's Messenger saying, "The example of a Mujahid in Allah's Cause . . . is like a person who fasts and prays continuously. Allah guarantees that He will admit the Mujahid in His Cause into Paradise if he is killed, otherwise He will return him to his home safely with rewards and war booty." (Sahih al-Bukhari 4.52.46)

A pithy hadith tells Muslims that jihad is the best thing in the world.

The Prophet said, "A single endeavor [of fighting] in Allah's Cause in the forenoon or in the afternoon is better than the world and whatever is in it." (Sahih al-Bukhari 4.52.50)

These are but five of hundreds of hadith in the canonical collections that clarify the nature of jihad in the foundations of Islam. Islam is built on Muhammad's teachings, and these teachings are contained within the canonical traditions. Simply reading the books on jihad found in these collections clarifies much. Appendix B includes many more hadith on jihad selected from *Sahih al-Bukhari*, Islam's most trusted canonical collection. I strongly suggest reading them for further study.

CONCLUSION

Although the average American Muslim agrees that the Quran and hadith are the ultimate basis of their faith, many have not critically read the traditions. Like me, they would be surprised to find violent, offensive jihad shot through the foundations of Islam. The Quranic revelations reflect the development in Muhammad's life as he moved from a peaceful trajectory to a violent one, culminating in surah 9 of the Quran, chronologically the last major chapter of the Quran and its most expansively violent teaching.

Surah 9 is a command to disavow all treaties with polytheists and to subjugate Jews and Christians so that Islam may "prevail over every faith." The scope of violence has no clear limits; it's fair to wonder whether any non-Muslims in the world are immune from being attacked, subdued, or assimilated under this command. Muslims must fight, according to this final surah of the Quran, and if they do not, then their faith is called into question and they are counted among the hypocrites. If they do fight, they are promised one of two rewards, either spoils of war or heaven through martyrdom. Allah has made a bargain with the *mujahid* who obeys: Kill or be killed in battle, and paradise awaits.

The summary in this chapter is not an alarmist attack against Islam or intended in any way to be polemical. It is simply an overview of Islam's foundational teachings on jihad with a focus on final orders. These teachings propelled a people to conquer much of the world at a speed and with a lasting impact arguably unparalleled in human history, save Alexander the Great.

Yet most Muslims today do not live their lives based on chapter 9 of the Quran or on the books on jihad in the hadith, and there are good reasons for this. We will discover why in the answer to the next question, "What is sharia?"

WHAT IS SHARIA?

WITHIN 150 YEARS of the advent of Islam, Muslims had expanded an empire from the Atlantic Ocean to India. Significant changes had transpired in their leadership and governance, as Muslims had also fought multiple civil wars and the seat of the caliphate had moved to Syria (see appendix C). It was at this time that Muslims began to record in writing the life and sayings of Muhammad.

Why had they waited so many years before doing so? The answer is not entirely clear, but it may have to do with the novelty of writing long works in Arabic at that time. The Quran was the first Arabic book ever put into writing, and the Arabic script of the seventh century remained too deficient to capture the richness and complexities of its text. Muslims' desire to write the Quran drove the development of the Arabic script. This is the charitable answer to the question of why Muhammad's life and sayings were recorded so long after his death; a growing opinion in scholarship is that the traditions were being fabricated, but I will leave that discussion aside.

Whatever the reason, Muslim biographers began to write about Muhammad's life around 770 AD. By 797 AD, the warrior ascetic Abdallah bin al-Mubarak had compiled his text,

The Book of Jihad, specifically documenting the development of Islamic warfare between Muhammad's day and his own. It was a precursor to similar books that would be found in the canonical hadith collections.

THE HADITH COLLECTIONS

By the middle of the ninth century, there were more than 500,000 traditions of Muhammad's life in written and oral circulation, and Muslim scholars decided to undertake the effort of sifting through them and distilling the most authentic accounts. Since the teachings of Muhammad are essential to Islam, it was necessary to distinguish accurate teachings from pretenders.

Among Sunni Muslims, who today make up approximately 80 percent of Muslims in the world, six collections of hadith are considered more reliable than any others: those of Bukhari, Muslim, Abu Daud, Ibn Majah, al-Nasai, and al-Tirmidhi. These are not the only collections used by Muslim scholars, but these collections are considered the most reliable, especially the collections of Imam Bukhari and Imam Muslim. The titles of these two collections reflect this, as they are called the "Sahih"— "authentic" collections.

Each of these collections contains at least one book on jihad, collecting Muhammad's purported statements about strife and warfare. These teachings are not presented systematically, however, but as collections of individual sayings or accounts of Muhammad's deeds. The systematization of these teachings ultimately came with the great Muslim jurists, and the formalization of sharia was the result.

WHAT IS SHARIA?

As I explained in the previous chapter, it is necessary to know the context of the Quran in order to understand its teachings. Islamic jurisprudence is the effort to understand all the teachings of Muhammad systematically, so that Muslims can know how to live. The end product, or the point of discovery, is sharia.

Put another way, Allah has given a code of conduct and a set of rules for all Muslims to live by. Following these rules is how one obeys Allah, thus securing his pleasure and living according to his created order. That is sharia.

The word *sharia* literally means "path" or "path to water." This imagery is strong, especially for a desert people. Following sharia is what preserves the life of the believer as water preserves the life of the thirsty.

Not just anyone can engage in Islamic jurisprudence, called *ijtihad*. Since there are thousands of verses in the Quran and hundreds of thousands of hadith, it is expected that only trained Muslim jurists can engage in determining what sharia teaches. The jurist must give primacy to the Quran, then consider the actions (*sunnah*) and sayings (*hadith*) of Muhammad, followed by reviewing the consensus of Islamic scholars, or *ijma*, before using his own reasoning (*qiyas*). By following these four steps, a Muslim jurist can make a decision, or *fatwa*, about what sharia teaches on a given matter. The ultimate goal is to apply the teachings of sharia to Muslim life, and that is called *fiqh*.

This process may seem straightforward, but there are many complicating factors that give rise to significant disagreements among Muslims. One such important factor is abrogation.

ABROGATION

According to Islamic tradition, as the Quran was being revealed during Muhammad's life, certain teachings and passages cancelled previous revelations. For example, most classical Muslim jurists were convinced that the verse of the sword (9:5) cancelled peaceful passages of the Quran such as chapter 109. This process of cancelling teachings is called abrogation, and classical Muslim scholars believed there were multiple kinds of abrogation, wherein either the text or the application of a Quranic verse has been cancelled.

Perhaps the most problematic category of abrogation comprises those Quranic commands that still apply to Muslims even though the text itself has been abrogated. In other words, the Quran is believed to contain teachings that are not found in its pages any longer. To find these teachings, one must know the appropriate hadith traditions. A famous example that hadith traditions record is the verse of *rajm*, stoning. Although the Quran appears to teach that lashing is the appropriate punishment for adultery (24:2), hadith indicate that a text of the Quran has been abrogated, but that the punishment of stoning still applies (Sahih al-Bukhari 8.82.816).

This feature of abrogation in the Quran, called *al-nasikh wal mansukh* in Arabic, is the great complicating factor in sharia. How is one to know whether a command has been abrogated? Is there agreement on when a command is to be followed even though its text has been abrogated?

SCHOOLS OF THOUGHT AND THE AVERAGE MUSLIM

Historically, not all jurists agreed with one another on matters of sharia, and they began to pronounce differing fatwas. Throughout the expanse of the Islamic empire, pockets of Muslims followed various schools of thought: Shafi, Maliki, Hanbali, Hanafi, or Shii. The last school was so different from the rest that it is now considered its own branch of Islam, the Shia branch, which leaves the other four as the major schools of Sunni thought.

The scholars in each school developed complex legal decisions and precedents, all building upon one another over the centuries. Until the twentieth century, Muslims often found themselves in one or another school of thought and had to take their civil or criminal matters to their respective courts for judgment. For example, the decision of whether a woman would be allowed to divorce her husband had to be made by a jurist in her school, and the different schools had different rules.

As is probably clear by now, at no point was the average Muslim expected to read the Quran to decide upon correct Islamic practices by himself or herself. Not only is Islam not a faith that upholds the sufficiency of scripture alone, the complexity of its foundations virtually necessitates a reliance on jurists and scholars for proper practice.

SHARIA AND THE APPLICATION OF SURAH 9

Sharia is not a book, and its laws are unclear until we reach the level of individual schools of thought. Even then, specific decisions need to be regularly explicated by Muslim jurists to this day.

Traditionally, therefore, Muslims have received their religion from their leaders and scholars. To assume that Muslims must live a certain way because the Quran or hadith command it misses a crucial step in the Islamic worldview, the distillation of sharia through Muslim authorities. If jurists and imams say that surah 9 does not apply to a Muslim's life today and that they should live peacefully with their Jewish, Christian, and polytheist neighbors, then it is entirely appropriate for a Muslim to follow his imam and live peacefully. Whether the imam is making the decision honestly or consistently is another matter.

CONCLUSION

Even though surah 9 of the Quran is very clear in what it teaches, and even though it is the final marching orders that Muhammad left for his people, and even though it strongly accords with the hadith on jihad, Muslim leaders in various schools of thought do not teach their followers to act upon its teachings today. Because of the expansive number of Islam's foundational teachings and because of complicating factors such as abrogation, Muslims do not determine fiqh for themselves but receive it from their imams. So they ought not be faulted for believing Islam is a religion of peace, especially if they have never confronted the violent verses of the Quran and the hadith. Yet the legitimacy of their personal, peaceful practice does not mean Islam itself is a religion of peace. We must remember that we are not defining Islam as the practice of Muslims, but rather as the teachings of Muhammad.

There is a tension between the reality of violent jihad pervading Quranic sources and the peacefulness of many lay Muslims on account of sharia, which I will return to ahead. Next I turn to another of the most common questions I receive: Was Islam spread by the sword?

WAS ISLAM SPREAD BY THE SWORD?

THE SHORT ANSWER: technically no, but indirectly yes.

As I have mentioned, different jurists began to develop codes of conduct with myriads of rules, but an overarching under-standing of jihad came to be shared in broad strokes. First, the world was to be seen as divided into two sections, one including those lands that were part of the Islamic empire and one that included everywhere else. The former is called *Dar al-Islam*, the house of Islam, and the latter is called *Dar al-Harb*, the house of war. A third division is also discussed at times, *Dar al-Sulh*, the house of treaty, where a treaty prohibited Muslims from conquering a land.

Second, in *Dar al-Harb*, fighting was not incumbent upon Muslims but it was permissible should they want the land for themselves. If they wished to conquer it, they were to first invite its people to Islam. If the people agreed, they were safe and the house of Islam was spread without the sword.

Third, if people refused to convert to Islam, they were then offered the option of paying *jizya*, the ransom tax. If they agreed, they were considered a conquered people whose lands now belonged to Muslims and they received the rights of second-class citizens, *dhimmis*. This option was given even to polytheists despite surah 9 of the Quran.

Fourth, if the people refused to accept Islam or pay the *jizya*, then Muslims could fight them. If the Muslims won, it was because they either killed their enemies in battle or because their enemies surrendered. In the case of victory through surrender, Muslims could do whatever they wished with their vanquished foes (Sunan Abu Daud 2612).

There may have been occasions in history when Muslims gave an ultimatum of conversion under the threat of death, but that was not the norm. A much more common outcome, for example, was the systematized enslavement of captives that Muslims then trained and enlisted as slave soldiers, or *mamluks*.

Given this process of waging jihad, it can be seen that the primary goal of jihad was not to convert people at the point of the sword but rather to expand Muslim territory. Conversion was one of the outcomes of jihad, but not its main purpose.

Yet if it had not been for campaigns of the sword, Islam would not have spread as widely as it did. As David Cook summarizes in *Understanding Jihad*:

> Islam was not in fact "spread by the sword"—conversion was not forced on the occupants of conquered territories—but the conquests created the necessary preconditions for the spread of Islam. With only a few exceptions . . . Islam has become the majority faith only in territories that were conquered by force. Thus, the conquests and the doctrine that motivated these conquests—jihad—were crucial to the development of Islam.

Although the object of jihad was not conversion, once lands had been conquered, people were more prone to converting. This is unsurprising, as second-class *dhimmi* status was at times harsh. Also, the *jizya* was not a set amount, and records indicate that it was prone to change over time. Conquered Christians record that Amr ibn al-As, one of Muhammad's companions, is recorded to have tripled their taxes, and elsewhere he raised the *jizya* until the conquered Christians were unable to pay (*Chronicle of John, Bishop of Nikiu*).

THE GOLDEN AGE OF ISLAM

It was through the injunctions toward *Dar al-Harb* that the Islamic empire expanded rapidly. Whatever the reality of that era and its warfare, many modern Muslims remember it with nostalgia as the Golden Age of Islam. Nostalgia is perhaps too mild a term; "longing" or "yearning" may more accurately convey the wistful sentiments of many Muslims. In their eyes, Allah rained his blessings upon the land because of the devotion of early Muslims, teaching them insights through the Quran that advanced them scientifically and intellectually beyond the rest of mankind. The world was as Allah intended it to be during this era when Muslims obeyed Allah and Islam reigned supreme.

This basic notion of supremacy through the practice of Islam appears in the Quranic concept of *jahiliyya*. The Quran teaches that, before the advent of Islam, mankind was in a state of ignorance and barbarism, *jahiliyya*. Obedience to Allah results in lifting mankind out of their base condition and into enlightenment.

The hadith build on this framework, coupling the proper practice of Islam with the generation of Islamic conquests. In a well-known hadith from Sahih al-Bukhari, Muhammad says:

> The best of you are my generation, and the second best will be those who will follow them, and then those who will follow the second generation . . . Then will come some people who will make vows but will not fulfill them; and they will be dishonest and will not be trustworthy, and they will give their witness without being asked to give their witness, and fatness will appear among them. (Sahih al-Bukhari 8.78.686)

The premise of this hadith undergirds the common Muslim conception of the Islamic Golden Age: after Muhammad will come the best era of Islamic history, and gradually through self-ishness and lack of integrity, Muslims will fall away from the proper practice of Islam. Classically, Muslims and scholars have considered the Golden Age to span 500 years starting at about the middle of the eighth century, but radical Muslims today are given to envisioning the era of the Golden Age as far back as the first generations of Muslims.

Those earliest generations are referred to as the *salaf*, the ancestors, and some fundamentalist Muslims make it their stated purpose to follow the ancestors' example. They refer to themselves as *Salafi* Muslims, and their hope is that, through obedience and integrity, Muslims can return the world to the Golden Age they have heard of and yearned for. Among their ranks is a strong propensity for radicalization.

CONCLUSION

It is easy to see why people would think Islam was spread by the sword. Muhammad said, "I have been ordered to fight against the people until they testify that none has the right to be worshipped but Allah. . . . [O]nly then will they save their lives and property from me" (Sahih Bukhari 1.2.25). Though this may sound like Muhammad wanted to convert non-Muslims at sword-point, early Muslims did not interpret it that way. Rather, it was understood that Islamic territory was to expand, but the fighting would desist if the vanquished converted to Islam.

This distinction between conquering for conversion or conquering them for their territory unless they convert is a subtle one, and in the long run the outcome was the same. With few exceptions, Islam is the majority religion only in those lands that were captured through jihad.

Muslims believe that because of the obedience of early Muslims, the Islamic empire expanded beyond all estimation.

The obedience of the earliest Muslims laid the foundation for the Golden Era of Islam, and it is remembered with yearning in the Muslim heart as a time when people obeyed Allah and Allah blessed the land. Mankind was at its pinnacle. Political, intellectual, scientific, and moral progress has never been sustained in such purity since that time. Muslims can thank the earliest Muslims, the *salaf*, for their devotion, and if they model their example in obeying Allah and following Muhammad with integrity, Allah will bless mankind again.

With these final pieces of the puzzle, the expectation of Islamic dominance and the nostalgic notion of an Islamic Golden Age, the foundations of radical Islam were laid.

Part 2

JIHAD TODAY

WHAT IS RADICAL ISLAM?

IN 1950 AN EGYPTIAN literary critic with refined sensibilities and a toothbrush moustache moved into a sleepy town in northern Colorado. The America he encountered, seen through the lens of post-colonial tumult and his devout Islamic upbringing, ultimately transformed Sayyid Qutb into the father of radical Islam.

THE BIRTH OF RADICAL ISLAM

As I have shown in my answers to Questions 4 and 6, the first Muslims were launched into a trajectory of global warfare with no clearly delineated endpoint. There was an expectation of Muslim domination that would be the result of faithful practice of Islam, including endeavors of jihad, which the Quran enjoins upon all good Muslims. The *salaf* generation exemplified obedience with their devotion and their conquests. In return, Allah blessed them with the Golden Age of Islam. At the risk of overgeneralizing, this common understanding of Islam boils down to this: True obedience to Allah will result in Muslim dominance.

The first cracks in Muslim dominance appeared in the mid-1700s, when Muslims like Ibn Abd al-Wahhab and Shah Waliullah noticed that Christian lands were progressing into what would become the Industrial Revolution. They began to ask themselves how it could be that Muslims might lose dominance, given the promises of the Quran. Hundreds of years later, these questions would drive the development of radical Islam. For the time being, though, the Muslims remained dominant over the vast territories that they had colonized.

The irony is that colonizing imperatives of Islam were put to an end by European colonialism. By 1920, every region of the Muslim world that Europeans desired was either directly or indirectly under European control. The foundational doctrines of Islam predicated upon Muslim superiority were now moot, and it became necessary to redefine jihad in the umbra of anti-colonial angst.

Abu al-Ala al-Maududi, a highly acclaimed Muslim scholar from the Indian subcontinent, attempted to redefine jihad in his 1930 work *Jihad in Islam*. As he was eager to denounce European colonialists for their rule over his homeland, he was obligated to explain how jihad was not a colonialist endeavor. Against the consensus of early Muslim jurists, he argued that jihad was not an effort to conquer lands, but rather a sincere desire of Muslims to spread the religion that they loved. It was through jihad that non-Muslims were able to encounter Islam. In other words, *mujahideen* were not colonialists but liberators and freedom fighters. His reasoning and apologetics were highly influential during his lifetime and remain so today.

One of the men Maududi influenced was Sayyid Qutb. Unlike Maududi, Qutb was not an apologist, and his writings are devoid of guile. Having spent a few years as a student in the United States, Qutb was repelled by Western society. Even though he had lived in a sleepy town in northern Colorado that was prudish by most American standards, he was horrified by American culture. He saw Americans as ill-bred, brutish, and savage. Their music was little short of screaming, their art was unsophisticated, and they were altogether numb to spiritual values.

By contrast, he viewed the Arab world as brimming with

Old World refinement and grace, especially when it came to higher matters of morality and spirituality. This enlightened condition he attributed to the blessings of Islam. America, by contrast, existed in a state of *jahiliyya*.

As the tendrils of the West were beginning to influence Arab politics, especially after the collapse of the Ottoman Empire and the establishment of Israel, the expansive resources of America and its influence in world politics concerned Qutb tremendously. He saw Egypt falling to the barbarous power of the West.

Upon returning to Egypt Qutb joined the Muslim Brotherhood, an organization that had recently been developed with the intent of starting an Islamic revival and returning to the study of the Quran and hadith. He quickly became the brotherhood's most dominant intellectual figure, infusing it with his thoughts and perspectives, until Gamal Abd al-Nasir's regime arrested him along with most of the brotherhood's leadership. Qutb was humiliated, tortured, and ultimately executed under false charges by a government that was, indeed, increasingly coming under the influence of the West. Because of the way the government treated him, many Muslims hailed him as a hero and a martyr for his message.

What was that message? Qutb believed Islam was the answer the world needed, but nowhere was it being practiced according to the principles of the Quran and Muhammad's life. The world was in disarray because democracy reigned in the West and communism in the East. Muslim rulers were courting these foreign governments and modern principles, abandoning sharia and making themselves apostates.

This is important to grasp: Qutb saw the leaders of Muslim countries as hypocrites and apostates, no longer following Islam. They were a large part of the problem. If Muslims would but follow the original, pure Islam, Allah would bless all the Muslims, the ummah, and return them to dominance. Muslims must thus raze centuries of accreted Islamic tradition and return to the teachings of Muhammad and the Quran. If they did, there would be a glorious revival of Islam for the betterment of the world, just as there was in Muhammad's time and during the Golden Age of the Islamic empire.

Qutb maintained a consistent approach to jihad, returning to the foundations of Islam for guidance. Jihad ought to progress in stages, just as it did in Muhammad's life. One should start by peacefully proclaiming Islam, then engaging in limited warfare, then exacting retribution for injustices against the Islamic community, and finally launching in warfare without end against the non-Muslim world. However, under the influence of Maududi, Qutb envisioned jihad as a liberation of the non-Muslim's mind, ensuring that the non-Muslim is able to hear and consider the message of Islam, something that may not happen unless jihad is waged.

Qutb's martyrdom fanned his popularity among Egyptians, even though many Arabs also maintained hopes that modernization would benefit their nations as it had the Soviet Union and the West. When Israel decimated the Arab coalition of Egypt, Jordan, and Syria during the Six Days War of 1967, these hopes were dashed, and many more Arabs began to sympathize with Qutb's views. President Anwar al-Sadat's negotiations with Israel a decade later added fuel to this fire, confirming in the minds of many Arabs that their leaders had betrayed Muslims and become apostates.

In light of this background, it becomes more understandable why Sadat was murdered in 1981. After his assassination, investigators recovered a document authored by Abd al-Salam Faraj. Faraj built on the foundation laid by Qutb by saying that Muslim leaders had become apostates and Muslims needed to return to a pure form of Islam, but he dispensed with Maududi's notion of liberation. Instead he espoused a more historically accurate notion of jihad: When Muslims fight non-Muslims, Allah will bless them and give them territory where they will be able to establish an Islamic state and reintroduce the caliphate. There, Islam could be practiced in the pure form that apostate Muslim governments were neglecting.

Faraj went so far in denouncing Muslim governments as apostate that he equated them with Israel. Their proclaimed allegiance to Islam was just a veneer, in his view, designed to gain the support of Muslims and actualize their un-Islamic aims. According to Faraj, Muslim leaders were actually rebels against sharia.

TAKFIR AND MUSLIM-ON-MUSLIM VIOLENCE

Faraj treaded a dangerous road, one that alienated him from many would-be sympathizers. Historically, Muslims had maintained a generous approach to *takfir*, the practice of proclaiming someone an infidel. According to tradition, Muhammad declared that reciting the *shahada* was enough to consider someone Muslim; whether they were lying or not would be decided by God on judgment day. Qutb's declaration of leaders' apostasy, amplified significantly by Faraj, swung the door open wide for internecine hostilities among Muslims. But where was the line to be drawn? At what point could someone be declared non-Muslim?

This was new ground, and Faraj and his ilk ultimately settled on three nebulous criteria: an open manifestation of unbelief, ignoring the implementation of sharia, and a refusal to engage in jihad for the defense of the ummah. When all three of these criteria were fulfilled, a leader or a regime could be considered non-Muslim. Fighting against them for the sake of Islam would then be a legitimate jihad, and the aid of Allah could be expected.

I have frequently encountered the misconception that if Muslims are fighting other Muslims, their grievances must not be religious. After all, they are fighting others "on the same side." Understanding Faraj's and others' radical approach to *takfir* should clarify this misconception; Muslim-on-Muslim violence can have everything to do with religion.

Surprisingly, the archetype of *takfir* is found in the Quran, and I have already touched on it. The Quran regularly accuses Muslims of being hypocrites if they are less than zealous in their obedience. Although the Quran usually suggests that Allah will be the one to punish hypocrites on the day of judgment, one verse is frankly contrary, correlating hypocrites to non-Muslims: "O Prophet, strive against the disbelievers and hypocrites, and be harsh with them. Their abode is hell" (9:73). The word for strive is *jihad*, and here we find a potential Quranic basis for Muslim-on-Muslim violence.

CONCLUSION

If we consider the words of the founders of the movement, radical Islam was born out of a frustration with the political inferiority of modern Muslim nations to Western and Eastern superpowers, especially in light of the Quranic promise that Allah will grant victory to those who strive for him. Radical Muslims believe another Golden Age awaits Muslims who are devoted to following the true teachings of Islam, and they are zealous to bring this about and see the glory of Islam restored.

Radical Islam, then, grows out of an understanding that the average expression of Islam today is too far removed from the teachings of Muhammad and the Quran. Adherents often consider moderate Muslims to be apostates because of their lack of zeal for the original teachings of Islam, and the Quran lays the foundation for undertaking jihad against these hypocritical Muslims.

But to fully grasp what radical Islam is, we need to answer another common question: Does Islam need a reformation?

DOES ISLAM NEED
A REFORMATION?

I HAVE HEARD MANY PEOPLE, frustrated by the increasing frequency and scale of Islamist terrorism, suggest that Islam needs a reformation. What they may not realize is that radical Islam is the Islamic reformation.

This might sound shocking, but consider: Just as the Protestant Reformation was an attempt to raze centuries of Catholic tradition and return to the canonical texts, so radical Islam is an attempt to raze centuries of traditions of various schools of Islamic thought and return to the canonical texts of the Quran and Muhammad's life.

This desire to return to the original form of Islam can be seen not only in the words of Sayyid Qutb, but also in his method. He focused almost entirely on references to the Quran. It is true also of the Muslim Brotherhood and ISIS today, whose publications and proclamations are punctuated by references to the Quran and hadith literature. Radical Muslim organizations are explicit in their aim to reform Islam.

MODERATE MUSLIM SCHOLARS VERSUS ISIS

This reality became stark to me when I read an open letter written by 120 Muslim scholars rebuking ISIS for their version of Islam (see www.lettertobaghdadi.com). The letter starts with twenty-four points of "Executive Summary," the very first point of which emphasizes that "fatwas must follow Islamic legal theory as defined in the Classical texts." But ISIS does not grant authority to the legal theory of classical texts, the thoughts of the great Islamic jurists. They are returning to the foundational texts, the Quran and the hadith. The same is true for virtually all radical Muslim groups. This letter was therefore impotent in bringing about any change within ISIS, as I am inclined to think its writers must have known before issuing it.

Yet one of the points of the letter shot so wide of the mark that I am surprised it was included. In the writers' condemnation of sex slavery, unable to provide a single reference that Islam forbade the practice, they instead appealed to a modern consensus: "After a century of Muslim consensus on the prohibition of slavery, you have violated this; you have taken women as concubines and thus revived strife and sedition (fitnah), and corruption and lewdness on the earth. You have resuscitated something that the Shari'ah has worked tirelessly to undo and has been considered forbidden by consensus for over a century." I can imagine ISIS leaders laughing as they read this. Their whole purpose is to work against any consensus of modern Muslim scholars, especially if it contravenes the Quran and the example of Muhammad.

Truth be told, the Quran and hadith contain many references to sex slavery. The Quran explicitly allows Muslim men to use their captive women for sex (23:6; 33:50; 70.30). The canonical hadith collections corroborate the practice, going so far as allowing it even if captive women are already married and their husbands remain alive, or if the women are about to be sold and could be impregnated (Sahih Bukhari 4138; Sahih Muslim 3371 and 3384; Sunan Abu Daud 2150). The Quran also explicitly confirms the former practice, teaching that captive women can be used as sex slaves even if they are married (4:24). The "century of Muslim consensus on the prohibition of slavery" is a departure from the foundations of Islam, and radical Islam is against such *bidah*, innovations in Islam.

To be clear, I am not arguing here against the legitimacy of an Islam that departs from its roots, but as long as Muslims try to return to the foundations of Islam, such modern consensuses will hold little authority over the teachings of the Quran and the example of Muhammad's life. It is clear why ISIS does what it is doing; they are a part of the Islamic reformation.

PROGRESSIVE ISLAM

The notion that reformation should lead to peaceful expressions of a religion is predicated on the assumption that the origins of that religion are peaceful. As I have demonstrated, that is not the case with Islam. Since violence is built into the very origins of Islam, the religion would need to be re-envisioned in order to produce a peaceful religion that is internally consistent. Emphasis would have to be drawn away from the Quran and Muhammad's life, or the records of their contexts would need to be disavowed. This would not be a reformation but a progression of Islam.

Some Muslim thinkers have aimed to do just this. Fazlur Rahman, a Pakistani theologian of the mid-twentieth century, tried to impose humanist thought upon an Islamic framework, focusing on ethics and freedom. His method was to reconsider the historical authenticity of hadith, an essential component of the traditional foundations of Islam. He argued that hadith were formalized in the context of a living oral tradition; therefore, behavioral norms of Muslims of the time were formulated into the words and teachings of Muhammad. In other words, according to Rahman what we know as hadith are often simply the practices of ninth-century Muslims that have been petrified into an unchanging set of rules for all Muslims. Dispensing with the traditional foundations of Islam, Rahman offers novel understandings of the Quranic text, attempting to revolutionize the application of Islam.

Although this method might work in theory, Muslim culture tends to be too loyal to its heritage to allow for such a radical departure from tradition. Rahman was effectively exiled from Pakistan as an enemy of Islam. His continued his work in a context more amenable to progressive Islam, the United States.

Rahman has passed away, and other Muslim scholars have taken up his mantle. One of his champions is Professor Ebrahim Moosa at Duke University, under whom I had the privilege to study sharia for a short time. He and other Muslim scholars like him do not hesitate to denounce Islamic terrorism and to explore how Islam can be shaped to speak to our twenty-first-century context. In *Islam and the Modern World*, coedited with Jeffrey Kenney, Moosa asks questions like, "What happens when the sacred book and the world seem to contradict one another?" He proposed an answer to this question in one of his lectures. Even early authorities of Sunni Islam altered the practice of Islam to fit their contexts. Umar, the companion of Muhammad and the second caliph of Islam, did not apply the Quranic mandate of giving his soldiers a percentage of the spoils of war booty. He decided to give them a salary instead, reshaping the practice of Islam to fit the needs of his context. If Umar was appointed by Allah, as Sunnis believe, and he could reframe a direct injunction of the Quran to fit his context, can we not do the same today as responsible Muslims?

In like manner, some Muslim thought leaders are attempting to progress Islam beyond its origins. Yet the fact remains unfortunately true that they are working against the current Muslim zeitgeist, which is focused on the vindication of Islam by a return to its roots. Progressive Muslims have yet to obtain much of a foothold even in the West, let alone in Muslim-majority nations.

I hope I am wrong, but I doubt progressive Islam will ever have much sway among Muslims. Islam has always been grounded on obedience to Muhammad; that is the crux of the religion. Its cultural identity and religious practices are subsidiary to the commands of Muhammad, so the accounts of his life and teachings will always be foremost. Past successes of various schools of thought in progressing Islam away from Muhammad's example were partly indebted to the inaccessibility of Islamic traditions to the average Muslim. On account of the Internet, that can no longer be the case, as the traditions are a click away (see, for example, www.sunnah.com).

Progressive Muslim scholars aim to redefine Islam in its essence, to redirect its focus from the example of Muhammad to religious principles. Such a redefinition is far more difficult to accomplish than a reformation, which is why it is the latter that currently dominates the global scene.

CONCLUSION

As we reviewed in Question 5, the reason Muslims can be both devout and peaceful in spite of violent teachings in the Quran and hadith is that Muslim authorities have interpreted Islam in this manner for them, often in accordance with various schools of thought and centuries of accreted Islamic tradition. When Muslims wish to circumvent these authorities and return to the roots of their faith, whether due to disillusionment with current expressions of Islam or a desire to please Allah and win his favor, violent expressions of Islam are often the result.

It was this line of reasoning that led Sayyid Qutb to lay the foundations for radical Islam, and it was the same line of reasoning that led Abd al-Salam Faraj to intensify his view of jihad such that it became the cure for the ails of the Islamic world. The common denominator between these two founders of radical Islam was their zeal to follow Islam to their utmost, not as it was being practiced in the twentieth century but as it was established in the seventh century. Radical Islam is the Islamic reformation.

The endeavor to modernize Islam and make it relevant to

the twenty-first century is called progressive Islam. Progressive Muslim thought leaders, though few in number and limited in influence, are present and are working to recreate Islam's religious framework from within. Indeed, that is what it would take for Islam to become devoted to peace—not a reformation but a reimagination.

WHO ARE AL-QAIDA, ISIS, AND BOKO HARAM?

JIHAD HAS EXISTED for 1,400 years and is probably here to stay. That said, Al-Qaida, ISIS, and Boko Haram have been highly successful in their murderous aims, and their motives give us insight into their relationship with Islam.

AL-QAIDA

Translated "the foundation" or "the base," Al-Qaida has its roots in the Afghan anti-Soviet efforts of the 1980s. Near the end of the 1970s, the political atmosphere of Afghanistan was tumultuous, with Marxist leanings gaining strength and ultimately leading to the coup of 1978. The country's new president, Nur Muhammad Taraki, endeavored to bolster ties with the Soviet Union and initiated a series of modernizing reforms that actively suppressed traditionalists. Conservative Muslim leaders were arrested by the thousands and executed.

Had Western leaders been paying close attention to the development of radical Islam's ideology, they might have seen these circumstances as a pressurized incubator for growing radical Islam. Instead, after the Soviet Union deployed troops to Afghanistan and staged another coup, the United States and various other nations financed the training and equipping of Afghan insurgent groups. These insurgents called themselves the *mujahideen*, the fighters of jihad.

The United States allied itself with a man who seemed perfect for their needs, a mild-mannered and educated Saudi millionaire who was using his ties to the Saudi royal family and his own wealth to expel the Soviets from Afghanistan, Osama bin Laden. The United States and allied Arab countries funneled tens of billions of dollars in funds and weapons through Pakistan and into the hands of Osama bin Laden and other *mujahideen*. Bin Laden was even given clearance to establish recruiting offices in the US and other nations in order to recruit *mujahideen* in his fight against the Communists.

By the time the Soviets began withdrawing from Afghanistan in 1988, a faction of *mujahideen* under the leadership of bin Laden had split away from the rest because their goals were less political and more religious. Al-Qaida was born.

Only hindsight is 20/20, but this development should probably have been more foreseeable by those who worked with bin Laden. Shortly before being recruited by the US, Osama bin Laden had been studying the Quran and jihad at his university. The work of Sayyid Qutb had directly impacted bin Laden; in fact, Sayyid Qutb's brother and sympathizer, Muhammad Qutb, was one of bin Laden's professors.

It was understood that bin Laden engaged in charitable efforts, and perhaps that made people think his general outlook on life was loving and peaceful. But love for Islam is also what drove bin Laden to perpetrate acts of terror and what fueled his desire to liberate Muslim people from Western and Eastern superpowers that he viewed as enemies of Islam. It was his sincere religious motivations that were expressed upon the theater of world politics.

In response to questions of his followers and of ABC reporter

John Miller in 1998, bin Laden said, "The call to wage war against America was made because America has spearheaded the crusade against the Islamic nation, sending tens of thousands of its troops to the land of the two Holy Mosques." A desire to defend Muslim lands, combined with a mistrust of the Jewish people that is widespread and latent in Muslim cultures, is what drove bin Laden to target Americans.

That bin Laden's motivations were ultimately religious and not political is his own assertion, as he stated with great clarity in the same interview: "I am one of the servants of Allah. We do our duty of fighting for the sake of the religion of Allah. It is also our duty to send a call to all the people of the world to enjoy this great light and to embrace Islam and experience the happiness in Islam. Our primary mission is nothing but the furthering of this religion."

ISIS

The US responded to the September 11, 2001, attacks by spending the next decade systematically dismantling al-Qaida, an effort that was largely successful. The initial incursion into Afghanistan was hardly unwarranted, and America enjoyed widespread support from both non-Muslims and Muslims around the world as they attacked al-Qaida targets.

The same was not the case for the US's 2003 invasion of Iraq in search of weapons of mass destruction. Among radical Islamic groups the invasion was touted as obvious Western aggression, and their ranks swelled with sympathizers and supporters. Many Iraqi jihadist groups at this time consolidated around Abu Musab al-Zarqawi, who was given seed money by Osama bin Laden and who labeled his organization Al-Qaida in Iraq, AQI, as a sign of loyalty to al-Qaida.

Zarqawi's aims were different from bin Laden's, though, as Zarqawi was more interested in regional concerns than global politics. He focused on sectarian matters, mostly attacking

Muslim leaders in Iraq that he considered apostates, even those Sunni leaders who collaborated with Shia. This lost him a great deal of support among Muslims, and it kept Zarqawi's AQI a lesser threat to the United States than bin Laden's al-Qaida.

By the time of the Syrian civil war in 2011, the personalities had changed. US forces had killed both Zarqawi and Osama bin Laden. Abu Bakr al-Baghdadi had taken over AQI, and Ayman Zawahiri had ascended al-Qaida in place of bin Laden. Baghdadi capitalized on the chaos in Syria and sent Iraqi fighters to take part in the conflict, ultimately establishing an al-Qaida presence in Syria. For a variety of reasons, Zawahiri ordered Baghdadi to release the new Syrian division from AQI, but Baghdadi refused. This led to the split between al-Qaida and AQI in February of 2014, the latter now preferring to call itself the Islamic State in Iraq and Syria, or ISIS.

Four months later, Baghdadi's forces swept through Iraq and expanded further into Syria. They gained control of several important resources such as the city of Mosul, with its 1,500 Humvees and fifty heavy artillery howitzers that had been supplied by the US. It was rumored that ISIS even gained control of $430 million by taking over the banks of Mosul, though ISIS never confirmed this report.

In the wake of this tremendous success, ISIS realized the dream of Abd al-Salam Faraj and radical Muslims around the world: They announced a caliphate, with Baghdadi the obvious occupant of the ruling seat. This move, considered symbolic by some pundits and moot by many Muslim scholars, nonetheless garnered tremendous support within the radical Muslim community.

Thousands of sympathetic Muslims flocked to Iraq and Syria to join the idealistic cause. In the middle of 2015 it was estimated that 20,000 foreigners were fighting for ISIS, including 5,000 Europeans. Although official counts of ISIS fighters range between 30,000 and 80,000, the former number seems less likely as official body counts of deceased ISIS fighters released by the

US have now exceeded 20,000. The latter number of 80,000 fighters, released by the Russian government, is still conservative compared to Kurdish reports of 200,000 ISIS fighters.

The war against ISIS has moved into the realm of propaganda, as some governments are moving to call the organization Daesh. France and Russia began using the term as far back as 2014, and UK prime minister David Cameron suggested the change at the end of 2015. Part of the reasoning for this move is an insistence by some to ignore the relationship of ISIS to Islam. As Obama averred in a 2014 memorandum released from the White House, ISIS "is not Islamic . . . [and] certainly not a state."

A more legitimate reason to cease referring to ISIS as "the Islamic State of Iraq and Syria" is that its influence has moved beyond Iraq and Syria. The group openly conducted beheadings of twenty-one Christians in Libya. Even though ISIS currently controls one third of Syria and one third of Iraq, referring to the group by the lands it controls is proving problematic and might be a good reason to change how we refer to them.

"Daesh" is the acronym for ISIS as it is rendered in Arabic, "al-Dawla al-Islamiya fi Iraq wa ash-Sham," but since such acronyms are hardly ever used in Arabic, the term comes across as satirical. Although the word itself has no meaning, it is a pun with the word *daes*, which means "those who trample." The term can also sound barbarous to some Arabs, vaguely suggestive of *jahiliyya* illiteracy and superstition. It is no surprise that the term *Daesh* appears to anger ISIS, which has allegedly threatened to cut out the tongues of those who use it.

Regardless of how we refer to the entity, ISIS is the realized dream of many radical Muslims to reestablish an Islamic state with a caliphate. It certainly is Islamic. Any avoidance of the group's theological motivations can only harm us in the long run.

BOKO HARAM

Nigeria is by far the most populous African nation, with nearly twice as many people as the next closest nation, Ethiopia. Throughout the 2000s it was home to dozens of radical Muslim movements, including Boko Haram. Boko Haram, like ISIS, has a longer, official Arabic name. Roughly translated, that name means "People Committed to Muhammad's Teachings for the Propagation of Islam and Jihad." However, the group's more common name reflects one of its founding principles, which is that "secular education is forbidden." The founder of Boko Haram, Muhammad Yusuf, was a high school dropout who enrolled instead in Islamic schooling. Although he was quite articulate and learned, he believed that the earth was flat and denied the water cycle.

Yusuf preached largely to university students and disaffected youth, asserting that there were four true Muslims they should follow, among whom were Osama bin Laden and Sayyid Qutb. It is widely believed in Nigeria that the government did not interfere with Yusuf's teaching because many members of Boko Haram came from wealthy and influential families.

Although there were long-standing tensions between the Nigerian government and Boko Haram, until 2009 the over-all approach of the movement was innocuous enough to be described as quietist, uninvolved in political affairs. But the short fuse was lit when, on an otherwise normal day, police ordered some young men from Boko Haram to wear motorcycle helmets. The young men's refusal led to a confrontation during which several young members of Boko Haram were shot and wounded. Conflicting reports make it unclear what happened next, but members of Boko Haram clashed with police in pockets around the nation, leaving a thousand of their members dead. The Nigerian military then captured Muhammad Yusuf and executed him.

Boko Haram, now led by Abubakr Shekau, was spurred into wide-scale action and declared an official jihad against the Nigerian government and against the United States, the latter an apparent influence of al-Qaida. Boko Haram began targeting politicians and clerics for assassination, holding true to their founder's principles by also focusing on symbols of Western advancement, such as schools, hospitals, and churches. Their methods have evolved from terror attacks implemented by individuals, such as suicide attacks and drive-by shootings, to massive concerted onslaughts against whole villages.

The West has only intermittently noticed the death and devastation leveled by the group. The world reacted in horror in April 2014 when approximately 300 teenage students were captured from their Christian girls' school in Chibok. First Lady Michelle Obama delivered the weekly presidential address on her husband's behalf, assuring Americans and Nigerians that the White House would do everything it could to "bring back our girls." She held up a sheet of paper which read "#BringBackOurGirls" for social media purposes, though it is unclear what she hoped this would accomplish. In contrast to this outpouring of support, the West virtually ignored Boko Haram's coordinated massacres in January 2015. Boko Haram is alleged to have assaulted sixteen Christian-majority villages resulting in 2,000 casualties and 30,000 displaced residents. The lack of response from the West may have made little difference, however, as the earlier show of support for the kidnapped Nigerian girls has resulted in no tangible benefit thus far. In late 2015, one of the girls escaped Boko Haram and informed the world of the girls' fates: forced conversions, beheadings, point-blank executions, rapes, and sexually transmitted diseases, but no rescue.

Because of their brutal efficiency, whether heeded or unheeded by the West at large, Boko Haram has been dubbed the world's deadliest militant group. In its Global Terrorism Index 2015, the Institute of Economics and Peace at the University of Maryland concluded that Boko Haram had killed 6,664 victims in 2014, 600 more than ISIS.

For a time Boko Haram functioned as a counter to ISIS,

even announcing its own caliphate less than two months after Baghdadi claimed the seat. What caught many analysts by surprise, though, was Shekau's pledge of allegiance to Baghdadi and the Islamic State in March 2015. Boko Haram now refers to itself as the "West African Province of the Islamic State," and judging by the improvement of the group's videos and speeches, it appears ISIS's propaganda machinery is now at the service of its African sibling.

CONCLUSION

Al-Qaida, ISIS, and Boko Haram are interconnected, and they all interpret and conduct their politics through the lens of their religious beliefs. There is no denying that each group has political aims, but these aims are grounded in a religious worldview, and their actions are driven by religious principles and motives.

Each group sees themselves as champions of true Islam, applying their views on the canvas of global politics for the sake of Muslim societies. Their practice of Islam places relatively greater emphasis on the foundational texts of the faith than does the practice of more moderate Muslims. Their methods are based on the writings of Sayyid Qutb, whose teachings were almost entirely derived from the Quran, and Abd al-Salam Faraj, who focused on the life of Muhammad in addition to the Quran.

When leaders and media members insist that these groups are not Islamic, they are either speaking out of ignorance or intentionally engaging in propaganda. These three groups are dynamic expressions of the modern Islamic reformation, and their interpretations of the Quran and hadith, in terms of being devoid of accreted tradition, are among the most pure in the Islamic world.

WHO ARE THE TRUE MUSLIMS—VIOLENT OR PEACEFUL MUSLIMS?

I HAVE INDIRECTLY ADDRESSED this question in the past few pages, but it merits a direct response.

A month after September 11, 2001, when President George W. Bush asserted that Islam was a religion of peace, the Washington Post reported Jordanian cleric Abu-Qatada al-Filistini acerbically responding, "Is he some kind of Islamic scholar?" Although he asked the question rhetorically, it is relevant to point out that most of the people who repeat such statements about Islam are not Muslims, let alone scholars of Islam.

A survey of Islamic scholars clarifies the matter. Muslims are torn about whether Islam is a religion of peace, mostly along lines of geography and culture. Islam is proclaimed to be a religion of peace almost entirely by modern Muslims in conversation with Westerners. Yet from the very earliest era of Islam until at least the nineteenth century, Muslim theologians were largely comfortable with violence, even systematizing and codifying it.

ARE TERRORISTS MUSLIM?

I have heard quite a few Western Muslims say that terrorists are not really Muslim, but such comments are tragically ironic. Western Muslims who say this are engaging in the Islamic doctrine of excommunication, *takfir*, pronouncing Muslims to actually be non-Muslim. They usually make no reference to the doctrine of *takfir* itself and may have no idea what the word *takfir* means, yet they are claiming to be the true Muslims. When radical Muslims engage in *takfir* and pronounce Western Muslims to be non-Muslim, they do so in light of Islamic doctrine.

By denouncing their radical Muslim counterparts, these Western Muslims are attempting to be the new Muslim hegemony and to silence the voices of Muslims who disagree with them. It is a peaceful version of what radical Muslims are also attempting, declaring theirs to be the one true form of Islam. On one hand this is little more than propaganda, while on the other it can represent an unfortunate Muslim tendency to see one's own practice of Islam as the only legitimate version.

A 2011 Pew Forum survey titled "The World's Muslims: Unity and Diversity" asked Muslims in thirty-nine countries whether there is only one correct way to understand Islam or if there are multiple possible interpretations. According to the survey report, in an astounding thirty-two of those countries, "half or more Muslims say there is only one correct way to understand the teachings of Islam." In the remaining seven countries, no more than 58 percent of respondents said Islam is open to multiple interpretations. Even in the United States, only 57 percent of Muslims said Islam is open to multiple interpretations. This strong tendency toward intolerance of internal disagreement is, perhaps, reflective of why many Western Muslims are so ready to declare terrorists as non-Muslim.

Of course, radical Muslims often see Western Muslims as apostates as well, but their disavowals are more systematic and, arguably, more Islamic. Whereas Western Muslims denounce violent Muslims based on a perceived majority commitment to peacefulness, radical Muslims usually disavow Western Muslims on the basis of the latter not strictly adhering to Islamic law. Once again, the interplay is ironic. Western Muslims appeal to democracy to excommunicate radical Muslims who appeal to sharia.

There can be no doubt by any useful definition of Muslims that Islamic terrorists are Muslim. They worship Allah, they strive to follow Muhammad, they perform their Islamic duties, and they have great concern for the international Muslim community. Relatively speaking, they tend to place more emphasis on the foundations of Islam than do average Muslims in the West who proclaim that Islam is a religion of peace.

SO ARE PEACEFUL MUSLIMS "GOOD MUSLIMS"?

The radical Muslim emphasis on foundational texts and their disregard for centuries of Islamic tradition tend to resonate with Protestant sensibilities. In fact, Protestants often ask me if peaceful Muslims are "good Muslims" in light of the violent trajectory of the Quran and Muhammad's life. If radical Muslims are placing a strong emphasis on following the Quran and the example of Muhammad, does that mean peaceful Muslims who largely ignore violence in Islamic foundations are not being loyal to "true Islam"?

As I mentioned earlier, Muslims can legitimately practice peaceful forms of Islam. Outside of the Protestant "Scripture alone" perspective, most religions impute some authority to persons, and obedience to those authorities is a part of the faith. Just as a "good Catholic" is one who obeys the Pope and adheres to the traditions of the Catholic Church, so a "good Muslim" is one who obeys his or her teachers and adheres to the traditions handed down in the practice of Islam. For this reason, those Muslims who practice the peaceful Islam that their tradition teaches are being "good Muslims."

Perhaps the question Protestants intend to ask is whether an insistence upon peace is consistent with the foundations and origins of the Islamic faith. I have attempted to address that question head-on in this book: No, it is not. Muhammad engaged in many battles, both offensive and defensive, both provoked and unprovoked, leading the Muslim community in eighty-six raids and battles during the last nine years of his life. The Quran's final commands are found in surah 9, chronologically the last major chapter of the Quran, and they are the most violent commands of all. The name of the chapter, "al-Baraa," means "the Disavowal." Not only was the surah a disavowal of peace treaties, but in many classical interpretations of Islam it was also a disavowal of other peaceful verses in the Quran through abrogation. The chapter commanded Muslims to fight their enemies, even family members, even if they did not want to, even against those who had not fought Muslims, even in the face of death, and even if martyrdom was the result, as that would lead to their salvation. This was to establish Islam as the religion that would prevail over all others. These Quranic teachings launched Muslims into world conquest and domination, and Muslims insistent on peace today must either ignore or reinvent whole swaths of Islamic history and thirteen centuries of Islamic tradition to dissociate themselves from violent Islam.

Many peaceful Muslims do not do so consistently, instead simply ignoring some traditions as if they did not exist. In that case, though they may still be "good Muslims," they are not being consistent thinkers.

CONCLUSION

Islam is a diverse religion with many expressions, though unfortunately there is a demonstrable tendency among Muslims to assume only one legitimate interpretation of Islam. On account of this, many Muslims accuse one another of apostasy, whether peaceful Muslims disavowing radical Muslims or vice versa.

The reality is that Islam can be formulated either peacefully or violently, but violent expressions of Islam adhere more consistently and more literally to the foundational texts of the Islamic faith, the Quran and the hadith. Peaceful versions of Islam must reinvent traditions from Muhammad's life in order to be internally consistent, or they must ignore them outright. Regardless of which of these two options peaceful Muslims choose, the common assertion that violent Muslims are not truly Muslim is uninformed or even disingenuous.

WHY ARE MUSLIMS BEING RADICALIZED?

AS I MENTIONED EARLIER, some reports estimate that 5,000 Europeans are fighting for ISIS, and more are being recruited every day. There is no specific mold for those who leave home to join ISIS, as the three teenagers from Bethnal Green demonstrated. They were among the top in their class, they were popular, they enjoyed pop culture, their parents loved them, and they were girls. While there are no clear indicators of who will be radicalized or when, certain trends can be discerned.

In February 2015, the US State Department Acting Spokesperson Marie Harf suggested that a "lack of opportunity for jobs" might be a significant factor in radicalization and terrorism. If anything, the opposite seems to be the case. Many Islamic extremists are wealthy or have well-paying jobs. Princeton-trained economist Claude Berrebi published a detailed study in 2007 ("Evidence about the Link between Education, Poverty, and Terrorism among Palestinians") that concluded "both higher education and standard of living are positively associated with participation in [radical Muslim groups] and with becoming a suicide bomber." It appears that resources and education are factors that assist in moving young Muslims toward radicalization. This follows the pattern of Sayyid Qutb and Osama bin Laden.

Suraj Lakhani, a scholar of radicalization in Wales, suggests that the process is driven by religious concerns and a drive to bolster one's personal identity. In addition, he believes that radical groups such as ISIS are able to radicalize young Muslims directly through the Internet, and he cautions that young Muslims ought not be allowed to hear ISIS messages or interact with their recruiters.

Naturally, I agree that interacting with ISIS recruiters is a bad idea, but what the recruiters say may shed the most insight on the radicalization process. Although ISIS lures potential recruits with a variety of hooks, its strongest emphasis, drawing on the Quran and hadith, is that it is the duty of good Muslims to fight against the enemies of Islam and to emigrate to the Islamic State once it has been established.

ISIS'S METHOD OF RADICALIZING YOUNG MUSLIMS

ISIS's message is not an enigma, as the group has been publishing a professional-looking, glossy periodical. The Clarion Project, a non-profit organization dedicated to exposing the dangers of Islamist extremism, has been posting each issue of this magazine online (www.clarionproject.org), where you can read ISIS propaganda for yourself. The publication is titled "Dabiq," an eschatological reference to the location of the final battle between Muslims and the West that will usher in the end of the world.

The third issue of the magazine represents a prime example of ISIS's recruiting techniques. Although it glorifies violence in a manner that could appeal to a young man's curiosity, and although it appeals to the duty of Muslims to take a stand for the rest of the ummah, it does both by frequently and consistently referring to the Quran and hadith.

Some examples: The magazine appeals to the prospective

recruit to leave his homeland and emigrate to the Islamic State by quoting a hadith from the canonical collections; it urges him to realize that he is living in times that reflect those of the earliest Muslims by referring to Muhammad's life; it encourages him to take a step of faith by quoting the Quran; and it praises him for his obedience by quoting yet another hadith. All four references to the Quran, hadith, and sunnah are on the same two-page spread. Such is the frequency and intensity with which ISIS uses foundational texts to appeal to potential recruits.

The magazine even defends its use of severe, barbaric punishments by referring to a punishment meted out by Muhammad, as recorded in both Sahih al-Bukhari and Sahih al-Muslim. Muhammad ordered of captives that "their hands and their feet be cut off, their eyes be put out with hot iron, and they be thrown out onto (black stones) so they would ask for water to drink but not be given any water, until they died." ISIS used this hadith to justify their execution of prisoners, an execution that they documented with multiple pictures on the same page.

Finally, it is worth mentioning that the magazine explicitly enjoins potential recruits to undertake jihad by quoting multiple hadith, and it also quotes surah 9 of the Quran.

Although ISIS lures youth through a variety of methods, it radicalizes them primarily by urging them to follow the literal teachings of the Quran and the hadith.

THE INTERNET AND THE ACCESSIBILITY OF ISLAMIC TRADITIONS

As a young Muslim boy growing up in the 1980s and 1990s, it was impossible for me to look up a hadith unless I traveled to an Islamic library, something I would never have thought to do. Even then the hadith would have been in Arabic, which I did not know how to translate. For all intents and purposes, if I wanted to know about the traditions of Muhammad, I had to ask imams or elders in my tradition of Islam.

That is no longer the case today. The Internet has made the traditions of Muhammad readily available for whoever wishes to look them up, even in English. Some publications include the grading of various hadith, so that the average Muslim can know right away how authoritative a tradition is. The Internet is thus bringing average Muslims closer to the canonical texts of Islam than ever before, allowing them to bypass their elders and the centuries of interpretive tradition they may be passing down. It is greatly facilitating the reformation of Islam and the radicalization of Muslim youth, not just by functioning as a medium for propaganda, but also by allowing Muslims to see the foundational texts of Islam for themselves.

THE RADICALIZATION OF WOMEN

Women constitute one out of every seven members of ISIS. Their basic profile appears to indicate that they are more educated than the men and more reflective before joining the Islamic State. They are generally single women who travel to Syria and marry shortly thereafter. Some of the factors that radicalize young women are the same as those that radicalize their male counterparts: faith, identity, and curiosity. For them, however, there may be another factor: freedom.

Young Muslim women who feel stifled at home, often sequestered by strict parents or threatened with marriage to men not of their choosing, are promised the opportunity of choosing their own husbands if they run away to Syria. That promise has been fulfilled for some, such as the Bethnal Green girls who received marriage offers from a variety of men and were able to choose whom they would marry. The UK media reported that one of the girls married the well-known eighteen-year-old "Ginger Jihadi" from Australia, who was later killed in an airstrike at the end of 2015.

Regardless of these young women's desires, according to a reporter from the *Washington Post* who visited a refugee camp and spoke to women who had escaped the Islamic State, the end result was often less than they had hoped for. "Those women, usually drawn by romantic notions of supporting revolutionaries and living in a state that exalts their religion, can quickly find themselves part of an institutionalized, near-assembly-line system to provide fighters with wives, sex and children. . . . Many local women find the restrictions extreme, backward and terrifying."

CONCLUSION

The factors for radicalization include matters of identity, curiosity, and freedom, but these drives are all promised fulfillment through the performance of one's Muslim duty. The former might be lures for radicalization, but the foundational teachings of Islam are the means. In addition, many young Muslims are driven purely by a desire to be good Muslims and to see Islam restored to its former glory, motives that investigations often ignore. The common denominator of all radicalized Muslims is their ultimate choice to adhere more strictly and more literally to the foundations of Islam than most other Muslims.

ARE MUSLIMS TRYING TO TAKE OVER THE WEST WITH SHARIA?

IN A SPEECH THAT AIRED on Al-Jazeera in April 2006, Muammar Gaddafi said, "We have 50 million Muslims in Europe. There are signs that Allah will grant Islam victory in Europe—without swords, without guns, without conquests . . . [they will] turn it into a Muslim continent within a few decades. . . . Europe is in a predicament, and so is America. They should agree to become Islamic in the course of time, or else declare war on the Muslims."

This statement affirmed the concern of many conservatives in the West that Muslims had launched a demographic and ideological war, seeking to subvert Western law and culture to Islam. It sparked a conversation that has scarcely subsided since, primarily focused on two matters, sharia and Muslim demographics.

SHARIA AND WESTERN LAW

There is more than one way that people envision sharia being imposed on the West. A caricatured view is that sharia will be systematically implemented in the US such that it wholly supplants the Constitution. This, of course, is virtually impossible, and there is no explication of sharia law that would allow it to be systematically applied as the entire code of law for a nation. Sharia is not a document or a set of documents that can govern a nation. Even in Muslim countries that endeavor to apply sharia consistently and comprehensively, like Saudi Arabia, Afghanistan, and Iraq, there are always supporting charters or constitutions that outline the details of governance.

A more realistic concern of conservatives is that principles or precedents of Islamic law might become implemented in Western society. In November 2010, over 70 percent of voters in Oklahoma approved the Oklahoma International and Sharia Law Amendment, requiring courts to rely only upon federal or state precedents in their legislation and not upon international or sharia law. The proximate cause of this bill's popularity appears to have been the fact that sharia already had impacted American court decisions, even excusing rape.

In 2009, a seventeen-year-old girl in New Jersey filed for a restraining order against her Muslim ex-husband who had forced her to have intercourse with him despite her tears and pleading. Her marriage had been arranged in Morocco just before moving to the United States. The judge refused the restraining order because the husband had not been acting with "criminal desire or intent" according to sharia. The judge ruled that the teenager's husband "was operating under his belief that . . . as the husband, his desire to have sex when and whether he wanted to, was something that was consistent with his practices and it was something that was not prohibited." Though the judge admitted that the action effectively constituted rape in American law, he denied that the man was guilty.

The amendment for banning sharia in Oklahoma was fueled

in part by the example of this court case in New Jersey. Despite obtaining a 70 percent vote in favor of banning foreign precedents, the law never took effect. Muslim interest groups successfully challenged it for being anti-Islamic and unconstitutional. The US District court deemed that the amendment was not "narrowly tailored" and not "justified by any compelling interest."

SHARIA, ISLAMOPHOBIA, AND FREE SPEECH

Less pronounced among conservatives than the two concerns above, though perhaps more widespread, is the fear that Islamic culture will indirectly influence Western law. For example, sharia effectively bans any and all criticism of Muhammad and Islam. The biographic traditions of Muhammad indicate that he ordered assassinations of people who composed poems against him or his teachings, such as Abu Afak, an elderly man who took issue with sharia and its apparently arbitrary commands. After he was assassinated, a breastfeeding mother of five, Asma bint Marwan, lamented the murder, and Muhammad ordered her to be assassinated as well. These are but two examples of how the traditional foundations of Islam disavow free speech, and they shed light on why the international Muslim community is outraged by criticism of Muhammad. Such outrage is the appropriate response according to Muhammad's example. The same reaction extends to drawings of Muhammad and criticisms of Islam as a system.

The Organization of Islamic Cooperation is an international coalition of fifty-seven member countries that works to "safeguard and protect the interests of the Muslim world." It publishes annual reports of Islamophobia in the West. *Islamophobia* is a poorly circumscribed concept, ostensibly used to describe bigotry toward Muslims but many times simply an umbrella term to refer to any and all criticism of Islam or Muslims, real or imagined.

Through its annual publication, the OIC unabashedly lobbies against free speech, hoping to silence criticism of Islam.

According to the OIC, free speech protects people who "have time and again aroused unwarranted tension, suspicion and unrest in societies by slandering the Islamic faith through gross distortions and misrepresentations and by encroaching on and denigrating the religious sentiments of Muslims." In other words, people who criticize Islam are to blame for the unrest in Muslim societies. The OIC's proclamation is directly antithetical to one of the premises of free speech, which is that people must be responsible for their own reactions in the face of ideas or beliefs that anger them. The OIC's proclamation is entirely aligned with sharia, however.

Partially in response to the OIC's lobbying, many Western governments are considering laws that might limit free speech. In 2008, in direct response to pressure applied by Muslim constituencies, the European Union mandated that its nations combat "xenophobia" by making it illegal to incite hatred against a person based on religion. Although the mandate seems noble in intent, it does not clearly delineate where "criticism of ideas" ends and "hatred against a person on account of religion" begins.

My own concerns about sharia in the West lie in this third area, particularly concerning possible governmental restrictions on free speech. As this book has demonstrated, I believe ideas can be dangerous, even popular ideas held by millions, and I furthermore believe we ought to be able to discuss such ideas freely. Unfortunately, there is a growing mob mentality even in the United States that allows unpopular ideas to be shouted down and the people voicing them to be accused of closed-mindedness and bigotry. I would not be surprised if, in the next generation, certain unpopular ideas were made illegal through restrictions on free speech.

The OIC is not the only influential and wealthy organization trying to limit the free speech of Westerners; there are similar efforts far closer to home. CAIR, the Council on American Islamic Relations, presents itself as a moderate Muslim organization aimed at protecting the liberties and interests of Muslims in the United States. However, the United Arab Emirates has labeled CAIR a terrorist organization, and the US Department of Justice has judged them to be the American arm of the Muslim Brotherhood. CAIR actively engages in restricting free speech on American soil under accusations of "Islamophobia."

CAIR's use of the term *Islamophobia* is even more concerning than the OIC's, as they are willing to accuse Muslims who disagree with them of being Islamophobic. When Raheel Raza, president of Muslims Facing Tomorrow, attempted to speak out "against barbaric treatment of women by radical Islamists" by a screening of her film, *Honor Diaries*, CAIR intervened and shut down the screening. The treatment that Raza wished to criticize was, by and large, an implementation of sharia, so CAIR accused her of Islamophobia even though she is a Muslim.

MUSLIM DEMOGRAPHICS AND RADICAL ISLAM BY THE NUMBERS

Raza released another video at the end of 2015 in tandem with the Clarion Project. Called *By the Numbers*, it focused on exploring Muslim opinions and demographic trends. In the video Raza explains that the world of radical Islam can be understood through three "spheres of radicalization," each successive circle growing larger but less overtly radical. The first and smallest circle she calls "violent jihadists." This is the group I have been calling *mujahideen*, Muslims who themselves perpetrate violence and warfare. The total number of *mujahideen* fighting for ISIS, combined with those fighting for al-Qaida, Boko Haram, Hezbollah, and others, ranges from 160,000 to 450,000 worldwide, 0.01 to 0.03 percent of the global Muslim population.

The next sphere she calls "Islamists," Muslims who actively impose Islamic dominance by working within Western political and cultural systems. Examples include Hamas in Palestine, CAIR in the United States, and the Muslim Brotherhood in Egypt. The brotherhood has an explicit goal of establishing an

Islamic state with a global caliphate, yet it is given the freedom to pursue its aims of Islamic dominance because it employs non-violent methods.

The largest and broadest sphere of radicalization Raza calls "fundamentalists." These are Muslims who neither pick up arms nor attempt to overthrow governments, but simply "hold beliefs and practices that no doubt seem radical." Citing a 2013 Pew Forum survey of thousands of Muslims in thirty-nine countries, Raza reported that 237 million Muslims are in favor of capital punishment for apostasy, 345 million are in favor of honor killings as a punishment for illicit sexual relations, and 469 million want to be governed by sharia law, approximately half of whom explicitly support whippings and stoning. These numbers reflect only Muslims in the countries surveyed. Adding the opinions of Muslims in other countries such as India, Saudi Arabia, Iran, and China would increase these numbers.

Laws regarding stoning, whippings, amputations, and the like are found in the traditional texts of Islam, many in the Quran. These are the punishments associated with *hudud* laws, those crimes committed against God himself. Raza implies that support for these laws constitutes radical Islam.

Thus, according to Raza's categories, radicalism is prevalent in the Muslim world, depending on how it is understood. If we consider only *mujahideen* to be radical Muslims, then the number of radical Muslims might be as low as .01 percent. But if we consider those who desire sharia governance to be radical, then at least 29.3 percent of the Muslim world is radical. Raza seems to suggest we should consider the latter number as more reflective of Muslim radicalism in the world today.

It may go without saying, but I think the situation is slightly more complicated than that. In my experience, many who say they support sharia only do so because it is the "right answer" for a Muslim to give. They have romantic notions of what sharia is, and they do not realize exactly what they are supporting. This is reflected in the survey itself, as 469 million expressed a desire for sharia law, only half supported the specific laws that would come with sharia.

The same may have been the case when the Muslim Brotherhood rose to power in the Arab Spring. It was the summer of 2012, and I was enrolled in an immersion Arabic program. My professor was a young, politically oriented Egyptian Muslim. I asked her what she thought of the brotherhood, and she said, "We will see. They seem like good people who want to do the right thing, but we will find out." Egypt did find out. When the nation realized the reality of the brotherhood's Islamist aims, including its dictatorial means, the nation turned on them. The crackdown on the brotherhood was brutal. Voters in Egypt didn't know what they had asked for.

CONCLUSION

So are Muslims seeking to take over the West with sharia? I would be quick to answer, "No, but . . ."

"No," because the question implies a conspiracy among the average Muslim immigrant, as if all Muslims are part of a ploy to take over the West. That is untrue and ludicrous. In my experience, Muslim immigrants are simply trying to live life as best as they know how, as are all of us. For the vast majority, imposing sharia does not even enter their minds.

"But . . ." because many Muslims do entertain romantic notions of sharia and Islamic dominance. The Golden Age of Islam appeals to many hearts, and in the minds of most Muslims it is nebulously connected to sharia. Yet as Muslims in Egypt loudly declared through the swift ousting of their elected Muslim Brotherhood president, the average Muslim might not know what sharia really looks like.

Overarching all of this is the undeniable demographic shift: Muslims are coming to the West, and they are bringing their culture and values with them. My encouragement to those who fear Muslim immigration is that we should engage immigrants with love and friendship, sharing our views and our lives with one another. Part of the reason why Muslim immigrants in the West can become radicalized, as with Sayyid Qutb, is that Westerners do not help them to understand our culture and do not provide them with appealing ways of navigating it. Segregating ourselves from those immigrants with whom we disagree only encourages further disagreements and misunderstandings.

Instead of fearing Muslim immigrants, we should embrace them and be the element of change we wish to see. Had someone done that with Sayyid Qutb, the world might be a different place today. I suggest friendship rather than fear as a better way forward.

Part 3

JIHAD IN JUDEO-CHRISTIAN CONTEXT

DO MUSLIMS AND CHRISTIANS WORSHIP THE SAME GOD?

IN MY FIRST YEAR of medical school, a male physician from India approached me, offered the Muslim greeting of peace, and told me that he knew my mother. I returned his greeting, but I had a hunch he was mistaken. My mother maintains *purdah*, the Islamic practice of wearing a burqa and socializing outside the family only with other women. I found it unlikely a strange man would know her or talk about her in this casual manner.

On the other hand, he was a physician, he was from India, and he appeared to be part of the Muslim community. Perhaps he did know her? Upon asking further, he assured me that he did. I recall him saying, "She lives here in Norfolk, and she is from Pakistan, is she not? I see her every now and again in the hospital. She is a smart, very kind woman." That certainly did sound like her. My mother is very kind and smart, and she is from Pakistan. Every now and again she came to Norfolk for treatment, too, though she primarily went to the naval hospital in Portsmouth. He was wrong about where she lived, though.

We lived in Virginia Beach, not Norfolk, but the two cities are right next to each other. Though he was wrong about a detail or two, I concluded he knew my mother after all.

But I was wrong. As the conversation progressed, he told me that he had admitted some of my mother's patients from the emergency room. Apparently he thought my mother was a colleague of his, but my mother is not a doctor. Although we were both talking about the same role, that of my mother, we were not talking about the same woman. I later discovered there was a Dr. Qureshi in the emergency room at the children's hospital, and from then on I was able to inform dozens of people that, no, she was not my mother.

I see intriguing similarities between that conversation and the one our nation is having as I write this chapter about whether Muslims and Christians worship the same God. The question is pressing because the national conversation has grown controversial in light of the refugee crisis and concerns about jihad.

THE WHEATON CONTROVERSY

Wheaton College, a flagship of evangelical educational institutions, placed one of its professors on administrative leave on December 15, 2015, for "theological statements that seemed inconsistent with [their] doctrinal convictions." Five days prior, while donning a hijab and staking her position on a variety of controversial matters, Larycia Hawkins had written on Facebook, "I stand in religious solidarity with Muslims because they, like me, a Christian, are people of the book. And as Pope Francis stated last week, we worship the same God."

Wheaton's decision to give Hawkins "more time to explore theological implications of her recent public statements" ignited a firestorm of controversy. One strong voice in the fray was Yale Professor Miroslav Volf, a theologian greatly respected for his contributions to Christian–Muslim dialogue, who wrote in the *Washington Post*, "There isn't any theological justification

110

for Hawkins's forced administrative leave. Her suspension is not about theology and orthodoxy. It is about enmity toward Muslims. More precisely, her suspension reflects enmity toward Muslims, taking on a theological guise of concern for Christian orthodoxy."

Such a dialogue-stifling judgment from a highly acclaimed Ivy League scholar was surprising, but it served to illustrate the enormous tensions in Christian-Muslim relations. As a former Muslim, I have many Muslim family members and friends I spend time with regularly, and I often encourage Christians to consider gestures of solidarity with the hope that, somehow, this affection will trickle down to the Muslims I know and love. I have even recommended that Christian women consider wearing the hijab in certain circumstances, as well as counseled Christian men to consider fasting with their Muslim neighbors during the month of Ramadan, as long as it is clear these gestures are out of Christian love and not submission to Islam.

So without a shred of "enmity toward Muslims," I must say that I disagree with Hawkins and Volf. My position is that Muslims and Christians do not worship the same God, but given the complexity of the matter we ought to stop demonizing those who disagree with us.

WHY MANY CONCLUDE THAT MUSLIMS AND CHRISTIANS WORSHIP THE SAME GOD

For years after leaving Islam and becoming a Christian, I believed that Muslims worshiped the same God as Christians but were simply wrong about what he is like and what he has done. After all, I had been taught as a young Muslim to worship the God who created Adam and Eve, who rescued Noah from the flood, who promised Abraham a vast progeny, who helped Moses escape Egypt, who made the Virgin Mary great with child, who sent Jesus into the world, who helped the disciples overcome, and who is still sovereign today. Is that not the God of the Bible?

For that matter, the Quran asserts that the Torah and the Gospels are inspired scripture and that Jews and Christians are people of the book. The Quran tells Muslims to say to Jews and Christians, "our God and your God is One, and unto Him we surrender" (29:46). If the Quran asserts that Muslims worship the same God as Jews and Christians, does that not settle the matter?

For years I thought it did, and the great overlap between Islam and Christianity meant we were talking about the same God. Just as when the Indian physician was right about many details and wrong about only a few, leading me initially to conclude we were both talking about my mother, so I used to think that Muslims disagreed with Christians on a few details but we were talking about the same God.

I no longer believe that. At a certain point the differences go beyond details to essential matters of identity, and it turns out we are talking about different people. When the Indian physician said my mother lived in Norfolk, he was wrong about a minor detail, and we could still have been talking about the same woman. But when he said she was a doctor, it was not just a detail: he was wrong about an essential characteristic. It became clear that he was envisioning someone else. In the same way, the Muslim God is different in essential characteristics from the Christian God, which is why I now conclude they are not the same God.

This matter is further complicated by the distinction between role and person. In my conversation with the Indian doctor, we were talking about one role, the one filled by my mother, but was it the same person? Clearly not. In the same way, Muslims and Christians envision the same role when they speak of God, the unique Creator of the universe of whom there can only be one. But is it the same person? In my view, clearly not.

I do not condemn those who think Muslims and Christians worship the same God, because it is a complex issue. But the identity of the Muslim God is different from that of the Christian God in essential characteristics. The Quran seems to agree with this assessment. Though Muslims and Christians worship a God who fulfills the role of Creator, the persons they see occupying that role are quite different.

HOW THE CHRISTIAN GOD AND MUSLIM GOD DIFFER IN ESSENTIAL CHARACTERISTICS

Let's start with the obvious. Christians believe Jesus is God, but the Quran is so opposed to this belief that it condemns Jesus worshipers to hell (5:72). For Christians Jesus is certainly God, and for Muslims Jesus is certainly not. For this reason alone, no one should argue as Volf has done that "there isn't any theological justification" for believing Christians and Muslims worship different Gods. There is, and it is obvious when we consider the person of Jesus.

Another difference between the Islamic God and the Christian God is God's fatherhood. According to Jesus, God is our Father, yet the Quran very specifically denies that Allah is a father (112:1–4). In 5:18, the Quran tells Muslims to rebuke Jews and Christians for calling God their loving Father, because humans are just beings that God has created. So the Christian God is a father, while the Muslim God is not.

Similarly, when we consider the Christian doctrine of the Trinity, Islam roundly condemns worship of the Trinity (5:73), establishing in contrast its own core principle of *Tawhid*, the absolute oneness of God. *Tawhid* emphatically denies the Trinity, so much so that it is safe to say the doctrine of God in Islam is antithetical to the doctrine of God in Christianity. Not just different but opposed.

This last difference is profound. The Trinity teaches that God is not a person, but three persons: Father, Son, and Spirit. To assert that the God of Islam is the same person as the God of Christianity becomes almost nonsensical at this point, as the Christian God is tripersonal, two persons of whom Islam specifically denies in the Quran.

There is more to be said about the differences between the Christian God and the Muslim God, especially in terms of his character as it relates to jihad, but I will return to those issues in Questions 15 and 16. The point I want to make here is simply that the essential characteristics of God are different in Islam and Christianity. They are more different, in fact, than the woman the Indian physician had misidentified as my mother. In theory, my mother could have been a doctor, but the tripersonal Christian God cannot even in theory be the monadic Muslim God. The two are fundamentally incompatible. This is why, according to Islam, worshiping the Christian God is not just wrong; it sends you to hell.

WHY DO PEOPLE SAY MUSLIMS AND CHRISTIANS WORSHIP THE SAME GOD?

So how can people argue that Muslims and Christians worship the same God? Primarily by giving undue priority to the Islamic assertion that it is so. Even though the Quran says that worshiping Jesus or the Trinity will send Christians to hell, it somehow asserts that Muslims and Christians worship the same God (29:46). Though the logic is not clear, it is asserted as blunt fact that must be accepted. Ultimately, this is the reasoning of those who believe, as I once did, that Muslims and Christians worship the same God, and it is flawed.

The similarities between the God of Islam and the God of Christianity are superficial and at times merely semantic. Though Islam claims that the Muslim God has done some of the same things as the Christian God and sent some of the same people, these are minor overlaps and far less essential to the reality of who God is than fundamental characteristics of his nature and persons. Islam and Christianity overlap at points on the former, but they differ fundamentally on the latter.

Volf's rejoinder to this line of thinking is that Christians believe they worship the same God as Jews even though Jews do not worship the Trinity. How then can Christians say Muslims worship a different God without also saying the same of Jews? He argues that would be inconsistent or hypocritical.

Yet the response should be obvious to any who have studied the three Abrahamic faiths: the Trinity is an elaboration of Jewish theology, not a rejection. By contrast, *Tawhid* is a categorical rejection of the Trinity, Jesus' deity, and the fatherhood of God, doctrines that are grounded in the pages of the New Testament and firmly established centuries before the advent of Islam. The earliest Christians were all Jews, incorporating their encounter with Jesus into their Jewish theology. Nothing of the sort is true of Muhammad, who was neither a Jew nor a Christian. Islam did not elaborate on the Trinity but rejected and replaced it.

Additionally, Volf's assumption that Jews did not in the past worship something like the Trinity is debatable. Many Jews held their monotheism in tension with a belief in multiple divine persons. Though the term *Trinity* was coined in the second century AD, the underlying principles of the doctrine were hammered out on the anvil of pre-Christian Jewish belief. It was not until later, after Jews and Christians had parted ways, that Jews insisted on a monadic God. The charge of Christian hypocrisy is thus anachronistic.

CONCLUSION

The question of whether Muslims and Christians worship the same God is complex. Wheaton College made a reasonable decision in giving Hawkins time off to consider the implications of her statement. Whether or not she was aware of it, her statement allowed Islamic assertions to subvert the importance of essential Christian doctrine. Yet she ought not be faulted harshly, as these issues are murky. What is more dangerous is the path taken by Volf, accusing people of bigotry to shut down valid conversations. One can both love Muslims and insist that the God they worship is not the same as the Christian God.

Christians worship the triune God: a Father who loves unconditionally, a Son who incarnates and who is willing to die for us so that we may be forgiven, and an immanent Holy Spirit who lives in us. This is not who the Muslim God is, and it is not what the Muslim God does. Truly, *Tawhid* is antithetical to the Trinity, fundamentally incompatible and only similar superficially and semantically. Muslims and Christians do not worship the same God.

WHY DO SOME CHRISTIANS CALL GOD "ALLAH"?

IN JUNE 2014, hundreds of Malaysian Muslims rejoiced as their supreme court confirmed the illegality of Christians using the word *Allah* to refer to the Christian God. The Catholic Church had challenged the ban many times on the grounds that Malay Bibles had used the word *Allah* for centuries. Authorities argued in response that a Christian use of the term could cause confusion and entice Muslims to convert, a criminal act in twelve of its thirteen states.

For a time, the Church had succeeded in convincing the Malaysian government to lift the ban, but in response Muslims began firebombing churches, ultimately leading to a reinstatement of the ban in October 2013. Three months later, Muslim authorities confiscated hundreds of Bibles from Christians on the basis that they used the word *Allah*, and in June a seven-judge panel confirmed this hardline stance against Christians. Political pundits saw the ruling as a "vote-winner" for the government, appealing to a Malay public with sentiments that are increasingly Islamic.

ALLAHU AKBAR

When the decision was announced, Muslims around the court started chanting "Allahu Akbar." The phrase is called the *takbir*, and the Malaysians may have been reciting it simply in thanks to God and to give him praise. The slogan is versatile; it is used in daily prayers, upon hearing good news, during ceremonies, as an incantation before engaging in a difficult endeavor, or even in moments of general excitement. It is not primarily a war cry, as some believe.

So the Malaysian Muslims around the courthouse may have been chanting the phrase in celebration as many Muslims do. But if they knew the literal meaning of the phrase, they may have meant something more.

Many people think that *Allahu Akbar* means "God is great" or "God is the greatest." As a non–Arab Muslim, that is what I was taught the words meant. But the word *akbar* is actually in the comparative form, and the phrase ought to be translated "Allah is greater." It implies that Allah is greater than something in particular. Some have speculated that the phrase was originally used to intimidate the enemies of Muslims in battle, by saying that Allah was a greater God than their alleged god. In his earliest biography, we find Muhammad reciting the phrase before attacking the Jews at Khybar. This etymology is not certain, though, as there is not enough evidence to support it.

What is clear is that many Malaysians see *Allah* as a proper name for the Islamic God, so when they started chanting "Allahu Akbar," they could have meant that the Islamic God is greater than the Christian God. If they did, they might have been hearkening back to the original meaning of the term.

ALLAH: PROPER NAME OR GENERIC TERM?

Allah can indeed be used as the proper name for the God of Islam, but it also functions in most majority Muslim languages as the generic term for God. It is commonly believed that Christians used the term *Allah* to describe Yahweh even before the advent of Islam. *Allah* functions as a contraction of *al-ilah*, "the god."

So language and context matter when discussing the word *Allah*. When speaking in Urdu or Arabic, I tend to use *Allah* as a generic term, as do most speakers of those languages, but when speaking in English, I tend to use it as a proper name referring to the Islamic conception of God, as do most speakers in English. Those are just my preferences, though, and I would not hesitate to change my practice to serve a good purpose.

When it comes to suggestions for how others should use the term, I would simply enjoin them not to be quick to criticize. The term can be used in multiple ways, and our conversations would be far better served by focusing on meaningful matters rather than proper use of a term that can be legitimately used in many ways.

CONCLUSION

Some Christians call God Allah because it is often the generic word for God in Muslim-majority languages. I do not believe there is anything wrong with Christians adopting this word or other Arabic terminology if it helps clarify matters or build bridges of discussion, so long as it is not perceived as deceptive or confusing. Language is a fluid tool designed to help people communicate, and we should not be overly critical when others do not use terms the way we do.

HOW DOES JIHAD COMPARE WITH OLD TESTAMENT WARFARE?

NO MATTER THE CONTEXT in which I discuss jihad, one question invariably arises: How can one condemn jihad in light of the violence in the Old Testament? It is one of the most common questions I have encountered since jihad was cast into the public limelight. In fact, I had to address this question the morning I wrote this chapter, during a question and answer session in Atlanta.

I do not wish to argue in this chapter that the God of the Hebrew Bible is better than the God of the Quran, even though I am a Christian and will not be able to keep this chapter totally free of bias. Nor will I seek to defend the morality of the violence in the Old Testament per se; others have cultivated that task far more thoroughly and accurately than I could here. For example, consider the 2014 book by Paul Copan and Matt Flannagan, *Did God Really Command Genocide?*

In this chapter I simply hope to compare jihad, the Islamic doctrine of warfare, to incidents of Jewish warfare in the Old

Testament. The two religious systems conceive of warfare differently, and only after we have understood the details can we analyze the morality and ethics of either.

APPLES TO APPLES

To begin, we must make sure we are comparing apples to apples. The Quran is a very different type of book than the Bible, and it is easy to confuse categories when comparing the two. The Quran consists almost entirely of Allah's words in direct address (with a few notable exceptions, such as the words of worshipers in surah 1). The Bible, on the other hand, contains many genres, including poetry, apocalyptic literature, wisdom literature, prophecy, and history.

This final genre means that the Bible recounts many events not endorsed by God, but simply recorded in God's Word. Such events should not be placed in the same category as battles that God himself commanded. The latter category is the one of interest for our purposes.

For example, I have seen many polemical discussions focus on Genesis 34. In this account, Jacob's daughter is raped by a Canaanite, and her brothers seek revenge by lying to the men of the Canaanite city and then killing all the males, looting corpses and houses, seizing flocks and herds, and taking women and children captive. Yet Yahweh never sanctioned this. It is inappropriate to consider this an attack that God had commanded. There are other attacks that Yahweh did endorse, such as the ones commanded in Deuteronomy 20:16–18, but we ought to keep these distinctions clear.

RULE NUMBER 1: WAIT 400 YEARS

I have a dear friend who once said, "If you want to follow the biblical model of attacking a land, the first thing you have to do is wait 400 years." According to Genesis 15:13–16, Yahweh said to Abraham, "Know for certain that for four hundred years your descendants will be strangers in a country not their own. . . . [I]n the fourth generation your descendants will come back here, for the sin of the Amorites has not yet reached its full measure." Warfare in the Old Testament was designed to purge the Promised Land of the Canaanites (a group of whom are the Amorites), and this was God's promise to Abraham. That promise was fulfilled 400 years later, affording the Amorites many generations to repent and change their ways before the Hebrews finally attacked.

This is different from jihad in the Quran. Although at times there were buffer periods of a few months before Muslims would attack (9:2), that was not always the case, as with the Muslims' attack on caravans. Additionally, the warfare the Quran commands is not due to any evil action, but rather due to the beliefs of non-Muslims, such as the Christian belief that Jesus is the Son of God (9:29–30).

THE CHOSEN PEOPLE

Another important matter to consider is that warfare in the Old Testament is not about subjugating inferior peoples. Yahweh does not promise the Jews that they are the best of people and that their enemies are less than they are. He makes this quite clear in Deuteronomy 9:4–6:

> After the LORD your God has driven them out before you, do not say to yourself, "The LORD has brought me here to take possession of this land because of my righteousness." No, it is on account of the wickedness of these nations that the LORD is going to drive them out before you. It is not because of your righteousness or your integrity that you are going in to take possession of their land; but on account of the wickedness of these nations. . . . Understand, then, that it is not because of your righteousness that the LORD your God is giving you this good land to possess, for you are a stiff-necked people.

In other words, the Hebrews were not inherently better than the Canaanites; they were a stubborn and stiff-necked people. Yahweh was not affirming the superiority of the Hebrews by giving them victory so much as judging the sins of the Canaanites.

The Quran, by contrast, envisions Muslims as the best people: "You are the best of all people, evolved for mankind" (3:110). It teaches that Jews and Christians who do not convert to Islam are the worst of all creation: "Those who do not believe [in Islam] from among the Jews and Christians and the idolators will go to hell. They are the worst of creatures" (98:6; see 98:1–5 for context). This is why the Quran in 9:33 commands Muslims to fight Jews and Christians, so that Allah may cause Islam "to prevail over all religions."

I must emphasize that I am not cobbling together verses of the Quran to make a point here, but rather am highlighting those verses that were used by classical Muslims jurists and theologians to explain the foundational teachings of Islam. This view of jihad reigned from the tenth until the nineteenth centuries, which leads to the final, most important matter for our consideration.

A TRAJECTORY OF DOMINATION VERSUS A TRAJECTORY OF GRACE

As I explained in my answers to Questions 4 to 6, it is not just that battles are memorialized in the Quran, but also that the final chapter of the Quran is the most violent of all, commanding Muslims to fight and subdue non-Muslims. The title of the chapter is "the Disavowal," and it disavows all treaties of peace that came before it.

Muhammad's life moved from peaceful to violent in a crescendo, reflecting the trajectory of the Quran, and he died just after conquering the Arabian Peninsula. His words in the canonical collections were, "I have been ordered by Allah to fight against the people until they testify that none has the right to be worshiped but Allah and that Muhammad is Allah's Messenger. . . . [O]nly then will they save their lives and property from me" (Sahih Bukhari 1.2.25). Muslims are commanded to follow Muhammad's example, and his example was jihad.

By contrast, the stories in the Old Testament do not enjoin Jews or Christians to fight today. Though commands to fight are recorded in the text, no Jew or Christian is commanded to memorialize these battles as ongoing conduct. They were a part of the history of Israel, certainly, but not a mandate or continuing command going forward.

Although I cannot speak fairly for the various branches of Judaism, I can speak for the Christian faith: Jesus is the exemplar of Christians, and his message was one of grace and love. The violent stories in the Old Testament, however we understand their moral justification, serve as little more than a historical footnote in the practice and expectation of the Christian life.

CONCLUSION

This question deserves much deeper treatment than I can give it here, especially the presence of God's grace even in the Old Testament and Jesus' role in present and eschatological judgment. But when we compare apples to apples, we see that there is a great difference between jihad and violence in the Old Testament. An increasing trajectory of jihad was the model of Muhammad until the day he died, and he is the exemplar for Muslims. It was enjoined upon them, the best people in mankind, in the final commands of the Quran so that Islam could prevail over all other religions. Early and classical Muslims interpreted jihad accordingly, systematizing it into a doctrine and ultimately coming to dominate one-third of the known world.

By contrast, the violence in the Old Testament that God commanded occurred after 400 years of waiting. God reminded the Jews that the expulsion of other races was not because the Jews were the best of people but because others had sinned.

Ultimately, Old Testament warfare is not meant to be an example that Christians model their lives around today. The trajectory in Christianity is not from peaceful to violent, but vice versa.

Violence has a very different place in Islam and Christianity's theological frameworks. The final marching order of Islam is jihad. The final marching orders of Christians are grace and love. I will turn to those orders now.

WHAT DOES JESUS TEACH ABOUT VIOLENCE?

ISLAM APPEARS TO ENVISION MOSES as a prefiguring of Muhammad, and there are parallels between the two men. Both proclaimed monotheism in polytheistic contexts, both led their people out of physical oppression, both guided their people in times of battle, and both brought intricate laws to their followers.

Yet Jesus did none of these things. In the four accounts of Jesus' life that we have in the Gospels, Jesus never led an army, never struck a man, and never even wielded a sword. In fact, his teaching on violence was clearly the opposite. The only place in the Gospels where we might expect Jesus to fight, during his arrest in the garden of Gethsemane when his disciples were willing to fight for him, Jesus gave them this command: "Put your sword back in its place . . . for all who draw the sword will die by the sword" (Matthew 26:52).

If Islam's final and most succinct commands on peace and violence can be found in surah 9 of the Quran, Jesus' final and most succinct commands on peace and violence can be found in the Sermon on the Mount (Matthew 5–7). This sermon encapsulates Jesus' teachings and forms a basis for Christian ethics.

Nowhere in the Sermon on the Mount do we find an allowance for Christian violence, even for self-defense: "I tell you, do not resist an evil person. If anyone slaps you on the right cheek, turn to them the other cheek also. And if anyone wants to sue you and take your shirt, hand over your coat as well. If anyone forces you to go one mile, go with them two miles" (Matthew 5:39–41).

This teaching works in tandem with Jesus' command to love one's enemies. Christians are not supposed to fight their enemies, because they are supposed to love them.

> "You have heard that it was said, 'Love your neighbor and hate your enemy.' But I tell you, love your enemies and pray for those who persecute you, that you may be children of your Father in heaven. He causes his sun to rise on the evil and the good, and sends rain on the righteous and the unrighteous. If you love those who love you, what reward will you get? Are not even the tax collectors doing that? And if you greet only your own people, what are you doing more than others? Do not even pagans do that? Be perfect, therefore, as your heavenly Father is perfect." (Matthew 5:43–48)

In the Christian worldview, the exemplar for followers of God is no mere man but God himself. Since God cares for those who are his enemies, even blessing them with rain, Christians ought to love their enemies and pray for those who persecute them, so that they can follow God's example.

This contrasts with the teaching of the Quran, where Allah tells Muslims, "O you who believe! Do not take my enemies or your enemies as allies, offering them your friendship when they do not believe" (60:1). Of course, that is not to condemn the Quran, as it is counterintuitive to love one's enemy. The Christian command may make little earthly sense, but it is the explicit teaching of Jesus.

There are no teachings in the Gospels that contradict this categorical command, none that abrogate the mandate for peace and replace it with violence or hate. Jesus' command is for grace and love, unconditional and unadulterated.

JESUS THE ZEALOT?

In his 2013 book *Zealot*, author Reza Aslan argued that Jesus actually did have violent aspirations. Aslan, a professor of creative writing at the University of California, Riverside, seemed to borrow heavily in his book from the 1967 arguments of S. G. F. Brandon that Jesus was a revolutionary figure seeking political upheaval and not opposed to violence. Arguments such as these, heavily criticized by the scholarly communities of both the 1960s and the 2010s, generally refer to a few verses to make their points.

One of the verses is Matthew 10:34, "Do not suppose that I have come to bring peace to the earth. I did not come to bring peace, but a sword." Those who quote this verse to demonstrate that Jesus was violent are either deceiving or deceived, as it is taken suspiciously out of context. The very next verse clarifies that Jesus is not talking about physical violence: "For I have come to turn 'a man against his father, a daughter against her mother, a daughter-in-law against her mother-in-law—a man's enemies will be the members of his own household.'"

Jesus is talking about division within families, not actual warfare. No honest and careful study could conclude that Matthew 10:34 promotes violence.

Another verse that can cause confusion if context is ignored is Luke 19:27, in which Jesus says, "But those enemies of mine who did not want me to be king over them—bring them here and kill them in front of me." Yet reading the whole passage makes the statement clear. Jesus is telling a parable, sharing a teaching about a king. He is not demanding that his enemies be brought before him and killed. Throughout the gospel of Luke, Jesus tells many parables, including ones about an evil judge who ignores a woman (Luke 18), a farmer who sows seeds (Luke

8), a vineyard owner who orders a tree to be cut down (Luke 13), and a woman who searches for a lost coin (Luke 15). These parables are not meant to imply that he is an evil judge who ignores women, that he is a farmer who sows seeds, that he is a vineyard owner who orders trees to be cut down, or that he is a woman looking for a coin. Similarly, his parable in Luke 19:27 is not meant to imply that he is a king who wishes to kill people. Rather, Jesus uses stories to provide memorable illustrations, and his parable in Luke 19:27 prefigures the outcome of those who have rejected God on the final day of judgment.

Perhaps more understandably, people sometimes turn to Luke 22:36 to suggest that Jesus considers violence acceptable. In this verse, Jesus says, "But now if you have a purse, take it, and also a bag; and if you don't have a sword, sell your cloak and buy one." It is sometimes assumed, since Jesus told his companions to purchase a sword, that he wanted them to fight.

Context is again critical, and a closer look reveals the problem with this understanding. Jesus in this verse is telling his disciples to prepare for a journey, and he suggests they purchase a sword among the list of items they will need for their journey.

The English word *sword* is also misleading here, as English speakers are prone to imagine a weapon used primarily for battle. The Greek word for sword that evokes such imagery is *rhomphaia*, but it is not the word for sword that Jesus used. Instead, he used the word *machaira*. Like a machete, a *machaira* was a long knife designed as a multi-purpose tool, useful for cutting meat or cleaning fish. Like a machete, a *machaira* could be used for fighting, but that was not its only or primary purpose. It would certainly have been useful as a traveling tool.

There appears to be confirmation of this interpretation within the text. As if to ensure that his disciples would not use the *machaira* for fighting, he tells them two are enough (Luke 22:38). Two swords could not be sufficient among twelve disciples for fighting, but they could be sufficient as traveling tools. Either way, the verse says nothing about actually committing violence.

The only remaining account in the Gospels that might suggest Jesus' approval of violence is his cleansing of the temple. Of all four accounts in the Gospels, the most apparently violent is the account in the gospel of John, which says,

> When it was almost time for the Jewish Passover, Jesus went up to Jerusalem. In the temple courts he found people selling cattle, sheep and doves, and others sitting at tables exchanging money. So he made a whip out of cords, and drove all from the temple courts, both sheep and cattle; he scattered the coins of the money changers and overturned their tables. To those who sold doves he said, "Get these out of here! Stop turning my Father's house into a market!" His disciples remembered that it is written: "Zeal for your house will consume me." (John 2:13–17)

This passage describes Jesus at his most zealous. He sees cattle and sheep sellers, dove sellers, and money changers, and he makes a whip for driving them all out of the temple. Some who read this passage might picture Jesus violently attacking people, but a careful reading shows that Jesus expelled all three of the groups differently, and none with violence toward people. First, the Greek syntax shows that he struck only sheep and oxen: "[He] drove all from the temple courts, both sheep and cattle." The sheep and cattle having been driven out, their sellers followed. Jesus then turned over the tables of the money changers, causing them to leave. Finally, Jesus did not release the doves as that would amount to stealing them, but he ordered their sellers to depart. So Jesus purged the temple of all three groups of people, yet struck no person.

CONCLUSION

For anyone who wishes to strictly follow the teachings of Jesus, there is no room for violence. Not only does Jesus never allow offensive violence, he explicitly teaches against self-defensive violence, living out this difficult teaching in the garden of Gethsemane.

This is a difficult teaching for Christians to grapple with, as it would otherwise seem self-evident that violence is permissible for just causes, such as self-defense or protecting the oppressed. I'm personally unsure where I stand in terms of pacifism versus justified fighting, but if hard-pressed, I would say that Jesus did not give us any exceptions. His commands were categorically peaceful.

Jesus' radical stance against violence coheres with the life he lived and the message he preached. The very crux of Christian theology is that Jesus, the example for all mankind, was willing to die for others, including his enemies. He came to serve those who killed him, even to die on their behalf. His commands to his followers are consistent with his example. He tells them to love their enemies, to pray for them, and to self-sacrificially serve them, and in this way to be like God. Reading Jesus' words carefully leaves no doubt: Jesus commanded total love and grace.

This degree of peace was so radical that Christians struggled even with the notion of self-defense, and for 300 years after Jesus Christians never fought a single battle.

HOW DOES JIHAD COMPARE WITH THE CRUSADES?

I WOKE UP RECENTLY to a tweet in which a disgruntled individual accused me of criticizing Islam inconsistently. If Christians fought in the Crusades, does that not show that Christianity is violent? If it doesn't, then how can I accuse Islam of being violent?

Of course, this individual did not have the advantage of reading the previous 16 chapters in this book before asking his question. By now it should be clear there is a great difference between jihad and the Crusades. Jihad was commanded by Muhammad and the Quran, both in principle and in reality, whereas Jesus commanded no such thing as the Crusades, neither in principle nor in reality. Therefore, jihad reflects the religion of Islam, whereas the Crusades do not reflect the Christian faith. There is a significant difference between the two.

HOLY WAR

As I mentioned at the end of the last chapter, Jesus' teachings on peace and violence were so clear that no Christian force entered into battle until after Christianity was assimilated into the Roman Empire in the fourth century. At that time, much that was culturally Roman coalesced with the Christian faith, and warfare began to gradually enter the Christian perspective.

By the turn of the fifth century, the question had become a serious one: Were Christians prohibited from all warfare, or might they engage in battle under certain circumstances? It was at this time that the Christian theologian Augustine began formulating a framework that would allow Christians to fight a just war. Providing stringent conditions, Augustine argued that fighting could fall within the will of God, but only as a necessary evil, an act that required penance. Many Christians adopted Augustine's view, and for the next few centuries some fought under the banner of their faith with the understanding that they would have to repent as a result.

So it was approximately four centuries after Jesus that Christians formulated a theology of acceptable warfare, but it took another seven centuries before Christians developed a concept of holy war. Just after the First Crusade was launched, the contemporary historian Guibert of Nogent remarked in his work, *On the First Crusade*, "God has instituted in our time holy wars, so that the order of knights and the crowd running in their wake . . . might find a new way of gaining salvation." No longer did warriors see themselves as committing sin when they fought; instead they saw their actions as meritorious, even salvific.

By contrast, Muhammad himself taught his warriors that fighting was salvific. According to Sahih al-Bukhari, "the first army amongst my followers who will invade Caesar's city will be forgiven their sins" (Sahih al-Bukhari 4.56.2924). As I demonstrated in the answer to Question 4, Allah essentially made a bargain with Muslims. Death in battle would secure a *mujahid*'s station in heaven (9:111).

So it was not until Christians were a thousand years removed from Jesus that they developed a theology of holy war, whereas Muhammad and the Quran themselves taught Muslims that fighting could be salvific. Holy war is in the very foundations of the Islamic faith.

THE NATURE OF THE CRUSADES

Some records of the Crusades depict Christians committing abominable acts. An example is Count Emicho's slaughter of Jews in the Rhineland. A rogue Christian leader, Count Emicho systematically slaughtered and plundered innocent Jews against the behest of multiple Christian bishops. He asserted that his zeal was on account of the Jews' mistreatment of Jesus, ignoring the fact that Jesus himself was a Jew.

Also jarring is the description of what crusaders did to Muslims after scaling the outer fortifications of Jerusalem, as recounted here in a translation of the *Gesta Francorum et aliorum Hiero-solimitanoruin* collected in R. G. D. Laffan's *Select Documents of European History:*

> Our men followed and pursued them, killing and hack-ing, as far as the temple of Solomon, and there was such a slaughter that our men were up to their ankles in the ene-my's blood. . . . Entering the city, our pilgrims pursued and killed the Saracens [Muslims] up to the temple of Solomon. There the Saracens [Muslims] assembled and resisted fiercely all day, so that the whole temple flowed with their blood. At last the pagans were overcome and our men seized many men and women in the temple, killing them or keeping them alive as they saw fit. . . . Then the crusaders scat-tered throughout the city, seizing gold and silver, horses and mules, and houses full of all sorts of goods. Afterwards our men went rejoicing and weeping for joy to adore the sepulchre of our Savior Jesus and there discharged their debt to Him.

At the end of the fighting, the archbishop of Pisa and the count of St. Gilles wrote a letter to the Pope, an English translation of which has been produced by the University of Pennsylvania, boastfully describing their victory: "If you desire to know what was done with the enemy who were found there, know that in Solomon's Porch and in his temple our men rode in the blood of the Saracens [Muslims] up to the knees of their horses."

Please allow me to be clear: I denounce these atrocities unequivocally. I am utterly against the courses of action that the crusaders took, as they demonstrated a disregard for the value of human life, a demonization of Jews and Muslims, and no grounding whatsoever in the teachings of Jesus.

That said, the descriptions in these accounts are clearly exaggerations, as there were not enough people in the entire world to create a knee-deep lake of blood in Jerusalem. We should not view this florid language as a precise fact.

We should also be careful to be accurate about the historical context of the battle. John Esposito, professor of Islamic studies at Georgetown University, has denounced the First Crusade in his book, *Islam: The Straight Path*, using these terms: "Five centuries of peaceful coexistence elapsed before political events and an imperial-papal power play led to centuries-long series of so-called holy wars that pitted Christendom against Islam and left an enduring legacy of misunderstanding and distrust." Professor Esposito's sentiments may be admirable, but they're based on fiction, a fiction that has taken hold of the popular understanding of the Crusades.

The reality is that Muhammad proclaimed war against Byzantine Christians, and his companions undertook the work of conquering Christian lands. Muslims had been subjugating Christian lands ever since the inception of Islam, just as the Quran commanded them. According to Crusade scholar Thomas Madden, in an article he wrote for the *National Review* shortly after September 11, 2001, "The crusades were in every way a defensive war. They were the West's belated response to the Muslim conquest of fully two-thirds of the Christian world."

This may bear repeating: Muslims had conquered two-thirds of the Christian world before the First Crusade. Islamic conquests were also often brutal. I shared one account of Muhammad's companion ordering his soldiers to slaughter defenseless women and children in my answer to Question 4; here is another example from the *Chronicle of John, Bishop of Nikiu* as Muslims were conquering the Bishop's people:

> [W]hen with great toil and exertion [the Muslims] had cast down the walls of the city, they forthwith made themselves masters of it, and put to the sword thousands of its inhabitants and soldiers, and they gained an enormous booty, and took the women and children captive and divided them amongst themselves, and they made that city a desolation.

This slaughter of men and enslavement of women and children follows Muhammad's example in his treatment of the Qurayza Jews. Let us also not forget that Muslims often enlisted the captured boys in their slave armies, starting with the *ghilman* in the middle of the 800s and later the *mamluks*. This practice became so deeply rooted in Islamic custom that, according to Daniel Pipes, sixteen of the seventeen preeminent Muslim dynasties in history systematically used slave-warriors.

CONCLUSION

When we condemn the Crusades, we ought to do so in light of what they actually were, a defensive effort after much of the Christian world had been conquered by Muslims. Yet I do condemn the Crusades. The slaughter of Jews in the Rhineland and Muslims in Jerusalem was unconscionable, especially since crusaders had taken on the name of Christ. If their efforts had represented the state and not the church, and had they been much more humane, perhaps I would feel differently. But to take the symbol of the cross, on which Jesus died for his enemies, and to turn it into a symbol for killing one's enemies in my mind deserves to be condemned.

As a Christian, I am thankful it took a millennium for Christians to so distort Jesus' teachings to support holy war. Had Christians engaged in such wars one hundred or two hundred years after Jesus' death, perhaps the matter would be less clear-cut. As it is, there is little question. Jesus did not commission any concept of holy war, and it took Christians a thousand years to depart from the foundations of Christianity radically enough to engage in it.

By contrast, violent and offensive jihad is commanded in the Quran and we find corroborating traditions in the life of Muhammad. The foundations of Islam command Muslims to engage in holy war, offering them salvation if they die while fighting. It took Muslims 1,300 years to depart from the foundations of Islam so radically as to insist that Islam is a religion of peace.

WHAT DOES JESUS HAVE TO DO WITH JIHAD?

JESUS IS SURPRISINGLY PROMINENT in Islamic eschatology. Not only do Muslims believe Jesus is a miracle-working prophet, he is also the Messiah who will return from heaven at the end of days.

THE MUSLIM JESUS AND JIHAD

The Quran underlies these beliefs in two passages. First and foremost in the mind of many Muslims is the understanding that Jesus did not die on a cross. 4:157–158 states, "[Jesus] was not killed, nor was he crucified, but so it was made to appear. . . . Allah took him up to Himself."

Yet the Quran also shows Jesus asserting his own death. In 19:33, Jesus says, "Peace is on me the day I was born, the day I die, and the day I rise alive." If Jesus did not die on the cross and was instead raised directly to heaven, how can he say "peace is on me the day I die"? Only if he will return to earth once more and die that time.

On account of these verses, the Quran is understood to teach that Jesus is currently in heaven, awaiting his return to earth, after which he will initiate the latter days and then die before the final day of resurrection. This belief is nearly universal among Muslims.

Furthermore, in the hadith Muhammad says:

> [S]urely Jesus the son of Mary will soon descend amongst you and will judge mankind justly; he will break the Cross and kill the pigs and there will be no Jizya. (Sahih al-Bukhari 4.55.657)

Also prominent in Muslims' view of the end times is a battle between Jesus and the anti-Christ, the *Dajjal*. According to Sahih al-Muslim, "The Last Hour would not come until the Romans would land at al-Amaq or in Dabiq." After this battle with the Romans, the anti-Christ will challenge Muslims and even have the upper hand against them until Allah sends Jesus back from heaven. Then, "Allah would kill them by his hand and he would show them their blood on his lance [the lance of Jesus Christ]" (Sahih al-Muslim 2897).

Beyond this point, Islamic eschatology begins to vary widely, depending upon one's denomination of Islam. Many Muslims believe Jesus will fight alongside Muslims, who will be fighting Jews, and even the stones will cry out against Jews on that day. Muhammad said, "The Hour will not be established until you fight with the Jews, and the stone behind which a Jew will be hiding will say, 'O Muslim! There is a Jew hiding behind me, so kill him'" (Sahih al-Bukhari 4.52.177).

Some believe Jesus will appear with another apocalyptic figure, the Mahdi, either equal to or superior to Jesus, but details vary among Muslims on these matters, and apart from these two figures are many other signs of the end of days. You might consider reading David Cook, *Contemporary Muslim Apocalyptic Literature*, for more information. Regardless of the specifics, however, it is a common Muslim view that Jesus will engage in jihad at the end of the world.

THE CHRISTIAN JESUS AND JIHAD

The Christian message, called the gospel, is this: God entered the world out of love for us, paid the penalty of our sins by dying on our behalf, and then rose from the dead as proof that he had defeated death. The word *gospel* means "good news," and it is the message that, on account of what God has done, we will live forever with him.

Since Christians will live forever, they are told not to fear in the face of death. Paul says, "Where, O death, is your victory? Where, O death, is your sting?" (1 Corinthians 15:55). Since we know we will be with God forever, there is no more fear of death for the Christian of true faith. In fact, death is even beneficial to a Christian, because it sends him to God, with whom he is longing to be. Paul writes, "For to me, to live is Christ and to die is gain" (Philippians 1:21).

The security of salvation is what liberates Christians to follow difficult teachings of Jesus and to self-sacrificially love one's enemies, even being ready to die for them.

That is why some Christians have been willing to go to tumultuous Muslim contexts and serve those who could do nothing for them, even in the face of death. Ronnie Smith was a Texan science teacher who decided to move his family to Benghazi when the Libyan revolution was underway. For a few years, he taught chemistry to high school students in the war-torn country, bringing them hope when they had little. He wanted to serve people just as Jesus had, and just as people killed Jesus, so a group of radical Muslims killed Ronnie Smith.

A short time before his death, Ronnie Smith answered a survey indicating that the gospel is what encouraged him to serve people despite the risk of death. He knew his life was in danger before moving to Libya, but Jesus enabled him to answer jihad with compassion. Through the message of the gospel, Jesus made Ronnie Smith invincible. He was able to love without fear.

Japanese journalist Kenji Goto went to Syria to rescue a new friend, Haruna Yukawa. Goto had met Yukawa six months prior, when Yukawa was trying to turn his life around after a failed suicide attempt following the death of his wife. When ISIS captured Yukawa, Goto believed there was a chance he could help rescue him. In an interview he said it was "necessary" for him to try and rescue Yukawa, and that his faith gave him the courage to go. Goto had accepted the gospel in 1997, enabling him to answer jihad with compassion. Jesus made Kenji Goto invincible. He was able to live without fear.

In February 2015, ISIS beheaded twenty-one Christians on a beach in Libya. In a video the men are seen moments before their execution, calling out to Jesus and mouthing prayers. Most of them were migrant laborers working in Libya to provide for their families in Egypt. Although ISIS slaughtered the men to shock the world with terror, the response of their families sent an altogether different message. In an interview with VICE News, the mother of twenty-four-year-old Abanoub Ayiad said, "May God forgive ISIS, . . . [but because of them] I gave the best gift to God: my son." The mother of twenty-five-year-old Malak Ibrahim said, "I'm proud of my son. He did not change his faith till the last moment of death. I thank God. . . . He is taking care of him." The mother of twenty-nine-year-old Samuel Abraham said, "We thank ISIS. Now more people believe in Christianity because of them. ISIS showed what Christianity is." The wife of twenty-six-year-old Milad Makin said, "ISIS thought they would break our hearts. They did not. Milad is a hero now and an inspiration for the whole world."

As with Ronnie Smith and Kenji Goto, these twenty-one men had been transformed by the gospel, as had their families. They were able to live and die with confidence, and their families were able to rejoice in their deaths because they are now truly alive. Bishop Felobous, himself related to five of the slain men, even expressed sadness upon hearing that the Egyptian military was retaliating against ISIS. "I was very sad when I heard the news of the air strikes led by the Egyptian military against ISIS. God asked us to even love our enemies." Even after they had slaughtered five of his relatives, Bishop Felobous was able to answer jihad with compassion.

According to numerous reports, one of the men on the beach in Libya was not an Egyptian Christian, but a citizen of Chad. It was not until he saw the faith of the men around him that he was moved to trust in Christ. When the time came to make his decision, asked whether he would denounce Christianity and live or proclaim the gospel and die, he said, "Their God is my God." He chose to live for one minute as a Christian rather than for the rest of his life after having denied Jesus.

CONCLUSION

Jesus has much to do with jihad, both in Islam and Christianity. In common Islamic eschatology, he personally wages war on behalf of Muslims, breaking all the crosses and killing all the swine. In this war Muslims will kill Jews and defeat them, and Jesus will destroy the anti-Christ for their sake.

In Christianity, Jesus shows Christians how to answer persecution with love. Although this suggestion might seem impossible to some and ridiculous to others, Jesus' teachings were always radical, and they are only possible to follow if the gospel message is true. If we will live eternally with God in bliss, then we can lay down this life to love even our enemies. In the face of jihad, the Christian Jesus teaches his followers to respond with love.

CONCLUSION

ANSWERING JIHAD

HOW SHOULD WE ANSWER JIHAD? This question is proving to be one of the more pressing and problematic of our time. If we avoid the truth about jihad, we leave the door open for innocent people to be killed in attacks like Paris and San Bernardino. If we lack compassion, we close the door to innocent people who need refuge from places like Syria and Somalia.

Responses to jihad in the past few months have been far too polarized. Some leaders have asserted that radical Islam has nothing to do with Islam, while others have seemed to assume that radical Islam is the only form of Islam. Both are dangerous responses.

As I have made clear from the beginning of this book, I am not a policy expert and I do not know how to end our struggles with jihad. But I believe I do know where we should begin, with the truth about Islam and with compassion for Muslims.

THE TRUTH ABOUT ISLAM

Islam is a complex religion composed of many facets and layers. The expression of Islam that shaped my young life taught me to love my family, to serve my country, to pursue my God, to repent of my sins, and to strive for a moral life. In addition, I was dogmatically taught that Islam is a religion of peace. But despite the many positive teachings and qualities, the reality is that Islam's foundations contain a tremendous amount of violence. The life of Muhammad and the text of the Quran are the two pillars of the Islamic worldview, and the traditions of each progress from peaceful beginnings to a crescendo of violent jihad.

Muslims are justified in moving away from the foundations of their faith either through centuries of accreted tradition or through an intentional reimagining of the religion. If they do so, they may be able to express Islam both peaceably and with internal consistency. However, as long as Islam continues to place primary emphasis on emulating the person of Muhammad and following the teachings of the Quran, without successfully supplanting the canonical texts and traditions, the end result will be the same. Islam will direct its adherents to its violent foundations with violent results.

Therein lies the problem, as almost all Muslims, whether violent or peaceful, believe they are following the original form of Islam. Muslims who study the canonical texts carefully will ultimately be faced with the inescapable conclusion that their foundations are quite violent, which is exactly what happened to me. I fought the conclusion for years, but when the reality became unavoidable, I was faced with a three-pronged fork in the road and had to choose apostasy, apathy, or radicalization.

THE ACCELERATED POLARIZATION OF MUSLIMS

This problem did not pose as much of a problem in past centuries or even decades. For the average Muslim it would have been a herculean effort to find and study these traditions, and most were shielded by received traditions. But the Internet has changed that, and any who wish to study the traditions of Islam can do so easily now with the click of a button. That is the major reason why, in my opinion, Muslim polarization has been accelerating: we have been seeing more apostates, more nominal Muslims, and more radical Muslims than ever before.

And with the click of a button, radical elements and recruiters can also present the violent traditions of Islam to zealous or curious young Muslims, compelling them to follow.

When perusing the propaganda of ISIS, one can see that they lure Muslims through many avenues, but the means of radicalizing them is nothing other than encouraging them to fulfill their Islamic duty by following the teachings of Muhammad and the Quran. Radical Islam's interpretations of these traditions are the most straightforward, with the most consistent use of the original texts and the most coherent perspectives in light of early Islamic conquests and formulations of doctrinal jihad.

Even though Muslims are often raised with the teaching that "Islam is the religion of peace," when they study the texts for themselves, they are faced with the reality that Muhammad and the Quran call for jihad. They will stand at the crossroads for only so long before they choose what path they will take—apostasy, apathy, or radicalization.

COMPASSION FOR MUSLIMS

As Muslims make that choice, it would benefit the whole world if they did not make it alone, or worse, with radical recruiters. We need to show compassion for Muslims and befriend them, not only because they are people who are inherently worthy of love and respect, but also because we can only speak into their lives and decisions if we have earned the right. I am not sure there is any way to intercept a Muslim at the three-pronged fork in the road, as there appear to be no markers or signs revealing the stage of a radicalized Muslim's journey until after he or she has made their choice. We have to be walking with them before they arrive at the crossroads.

This means being proactive, not reactive. It means living life with people who might be different from us. It means integrating communities and social circles. It means stepping out of our comfort zone and loving people unconditionally, perhaps even loving our enemies. And it means doing all this from a place of genuine love, not ulterior motives. Only then can we stop fearing those who are our neighbors, and conversely, only then can we identify those who actually do pose a threat. Otherwise we will remain behind a veil of suspicion and fear.

Fear is not a solution, as it will only alienate those we hope to deter from violence and it will serve as positive reinforcement to those who want to use terror. Fighting will not work, as it will only further convict those at the crossroads that the radicals' cause is just. Also, some specific radicals, ISIS, actually want us to fight back. Their hope is that they will sufficiently anger the world such that we fight them on the field of Dabiq, ushering in the end of the world, as the tradition of Muhammad foretells.

Fear and fighting, both fuel the radical fires. We need something that breaks the cycle, and I think that can only be love. Not love as wistfully envisioned by teenagers and songwriters, but love as envisioned by Jesus, a decision to engage others as image bearers of God, to put their needs and concerns above our own, even at the cost of our own.

I am not advocating naïve pacifism in the face of genocide and murder. Many Christians believe it is the duty of the state to fight for and protect its people, as defending the oppressed is an expression of loving one's neighbor. They often refer to passages such as Romans 13:1–5 and 1 Peter 2:13–14 to suggest that Christians should play active roles in such state-led efforts.

So I am not promoting pacifism, but neither am I advocating a violent response. I am, in fact, not advocating any particular course of action, but rather a frame of heart and mind that will, in turn, shape the way we respond.

That frame of mind is truth and love, and both elements are essential. Without truth we will not be able to identify the real problem, and without love we will not be able to formulate an enduring answer. Regarding the latter, I think the first-century theologian Saul was correct: even if we can fathom all mysteries and have all knowledge, it will not ultimately work without love.

Yes, I do suggest we share alternative worldviews with Muslims as one of our methods to address radicalization, especially the gospel. The gospel does not succumb to the pitfalls of fear or fighting, which only fuel radicalization, and it gives Muslims an appealing direction at the three-pronged fork in the road.

That is what happened to me. As I faced the reality of the violent traditions of Islam, I had a Christian friend who suggested that Islam did not have to be my only choice, that there was excellent reason to accept the gospel. Apart from the appeal of the foundations of Christianity, I can say from my own experience that atheism and secularism offered little draw as an alternative to Islam as they were not spiritually robust, a reality to which many Muslims are finely attuned.

ANSWERING JIHAD: A BETTER WAY FORWARD

The Muslim world today has, by and large, rejected violent jihad in modern contexts. Expansive jihad, as it was envisioned in the foundations of Islam and practiced in the early centuries of the Islamic Empire, is a relic of the past. But radical Muslim groups such as ISIS and Boko Haram will continue using jihad because of its expediency and the explicit mandates in the foundations of Islam.

Muslims today have unprecedented accessibility to the foundational texts of their faith, the life of Muhammad and the teachings of the Quran. Within those texts, they encounter a call to violent jihad. Unless Islam is reimagined and emphasis is drawn away from these traditional foundations, Paris and San Bernardino might be our new normal. Sadly, it is not likely that Islam will be reimagined soon, so we have to answer jihad as best we can.

My suggestion is that we engage Muslims proactively with love and friendship while simultaneously acknowledging the truth about Islam. This is not the final step in answering jihad, but it is the correct first step, and it offers a better way forward.

APPENDIX A

A SELECTIVE TIMELINE
OF JIHAD IN ISLAM

THE DATES LISTED are extrapolated from either Islamic traditions or from modern historical sources.

570: Birth of Muhammad
610: Inception of Islam
622: Flight to Medina / Starting Point of the Islamic Calendar
623: Muslims Begin Raiding Meccan Caravans
624: Nakhla Raid
624: Battle of Badr
625: Battle of Uhud
627: Battle of Khandaq
629: Battle of Muta
629: Conquest of Medina
630: Battle of Hunayn
630: Battle of Tabuk
632: Death of Muhammad
632: Apostate Wars
633: Invasion of Persia

637: Conquest of Syria–Palestine

639: Invasion of Egypt

643: Incursions into India

670: Incursions into Cyrenaica

711: Conquest of Spain

732: Muslims Defeated in the West by Charles Martel at Tours

1099: First Crusade

1187: Salah al-Din Defeats the Crusaders

1258: Mongols Sack Baghdad

1453: Byzantine Empire Falls to Ottoman Empire

1492: Spanish Inquisition and the Beginning of the Colonial Era

1683: Ottomans Defeated at Vienna

1918: End of World War I and the Colonial Era

1922: Dissolution of the Ottoman Empire

1928: Establishment of Muslim Brotherhood

1945: End of World War II

1948: Establishment of Israeli State

1948: Arab-Israeli War

1966: Execution of Sayyid Qutb

1967: Six-Day War

1979: Egyptian-Israeli Peace Accords

1988: Establishment of Al-Qaida

1993: Bombing of World Trade Center

2001: September 11 Attacks against the United States

2005: July 7 Bombings in London

2014: ISIS Establishes Caliphate

2015: Boko Haram Pledges Allegiance to ISIS

2015: November 13 Attacks on Paris

2015: December 2 Shooting in San Bernardino

APPENDIX B

MUHAMMAD'S WORDS ON JIHAD IN SAHIH AL-BUKHARI

BELOW IS A SELECTION of hadith from *Sahih al-Bukhari*. All the hadith are from the Book of Jihad, usually volume 4, book 52, but the numbering system has yet to be standardized. I have listed the below hadith by volume number and hadith number.

SAHIH AL-BUKHARI

4.43: Narrated 'Aisha: (That she said), "O Allah's Apostle! We consider Jihad as the best deed. Should we not fight in Allah's Cause?" He said, "The best Jihad (for women) is Hajj-Mabrur (i.e. Hajj which is done according to the Prophet's tradition and is accepted by Allah)."

4.44: Narrated Abu Huraira: A man came to Allah's Apostle and said, "Instruct me as to such a deed as equals Jihad (in reward)." He replied, "I do not find such a deed." Then he added, "Can you, while the Muslim fighter is in the battle-field, enter your mosque to perform prayers without cease and fast and never break your fast?" The man said, "But who can do that?" Abu-Huraira added, "The Mujahid (i.e. Muslim fighter) is rewarded even for the footsteps of his horse while it wanders bout (for grazing) tied in a long rope."

4.46: Narrated Abu Huraira: I heard Allah's Apostle saying, "The example of a Mujahid in Allah's Cause—and Allah knows better who really strives in His Cause—is like a person who fasts and prays continuously. Allah guarantees that He will admit the Mujahid in His Cause into Paradise if he is killed, otherwise He will return him to his home safely with rewards and war booty."

4.48: Narrated Abu Huraira: The Prophet said, "Whoever believes in Allah and His Apostle, offers prayer perfectly and fasts the month of Ramadan, will rightfully be granted Paradise by Allah, no matter whether he fights in Allah's Cause or remains in the land where he is born." The people said, "O Allah's Apostle! Shall we acquaint the people with this good news?" He said, "Paradise has one-hundred grades which Allah has reserved for the Mujahidin who fight in His Cause, and the distance between each of two grades is like the distance between the Heaven and the Earth. So, when you ask Allah (for something), ask for Al-Firdaus which is the best and highest part of Paradise." (i.e. The sub-narrator added, "I think the Prophet also said, 'Above it [i.e. Al-Firdaus] is the Throne of Beneficent [i.e. Allah], and from it originate the rivers of Paradise.'")

4.52: Narrated Sahl bin Sa'd: The Prophet said, "A single jihad in Allah's Cause in the afternoon and in the forenoon is better than the world and whatever is in it."

4.53: Narrated Anas bin Malik: The Prophet said, "Nobody who dies and finds good from Allah (in the Hereafter) would wish to come back to this world even if he were given the whole world and whatever is in it, except the martyr who, on seeing the superiority of martyrdom, would like to come back to the world and get killed again (in Allah's Cause). Narrated Anas: The Prophet said, "A single endeavor (of fighting) in Allah's Cause in the afternoon or in the forenoon is better than all the world and whatever is in it. A place in Paradise as small as the bow or lash of one of you is better than all the world and whatever is in it. And if a virgin from Paradise appeared to the people of the earth, she would fill the space between Heaven and the Earth with light and pleasant scent and her head cover is better than the world and whatever is in it."

4.54: Narrated Abu Huraira: The Prophet said, "By Him in Whose Hands my life is! Were it not for some men amongst the believers who dislike to be left behind me and whom I cannot provide with means of conveyance, I would certainly never remain behind any Sariya' (army unit) setting out in Allah's Cause. By Him in Whose Hands my life is! I would love to be martyred in Allah's Cause and then get resurrected and then get martyred, and then get resurrected again and then get martyred and then get resurrected again and then get martyred."

4.59: Narrated Abu Huraira: Allah's Apostle said, "By Him in Whose Hands my soul is! Whoever is wounded in Allah's Cause. . . . and Allah knows well who gets wounded in His Cause. . . . will come on the Day of Resurrection with his wound having the color of blood but the scent of musk."

4.63: Narrated Al-Bara: A man whose face was covered with an iron mask (i.e. clad in armor) came to the Prophet and said, "O Allah's Apostle! Shall I fight or embrace Islam first?" The Prophet said, "Embrace Islam first and then fight." So he embraced Islam, and was martyred. Allah's Apostle said, "A little work, but a great reward." (He did very little [after embracing Islam], but he will be rewarded in abundance.)

4.65: Narrated Abu Musa: A man came to the Prophet and asked, "A man fights for war booty; another fights for fame and a third fights for showing off; which of them fights in Allah's Cause?" The Prophet said, "He who fights that Allah's Word (i.e. Islam) should be superior, fights in Allah's Cause."

4.66: Narrated Abu 'Abs: (who is 'Abdur-Rahman bin Jabir) Allah's Apostle said, "Anyone whose both feet get covered with dust in Allah's Cause will not be touched by the (Hell) fire."

4.72: Narrated Anas bin Malik: The Prophet said, "Nobody who enters Paradise likes to go back to the world even if he got everything on the earth, except a Mujahid who wishes to return to the world so that he may be martyred ten times because of the dignity he receives (from Allah).

Narrated Al-Mughira bin Shu'ba: Our Prophet told us about the message of our Lord that "Whoever amongst us is killed will go to Paradise." 'Umar asked the Prophet, "Is it not true that our men who are killed will go to Paradise and theirs (i.e. those of the Pagans') will go to the (Hell) fire?" The Prophet said, "Yes."

4.73: Narrated 'Abdullah bin Abi 'Aufa: Allah's Apostle said, "Know that Paradise is under the shades of swords."

4.80: Narrated Abu Huraira: Allah's Apostle said, "Allah welcomes two men with a smile; one of whom kills the other and both of them enter Paradise. One fights in Allah's Cause and gets killed. Later on Allah forgives the killer who also gets martyred (in Allah's Cause)."

4.176: Narrated 'Abdullah bin 'Umar: Allah's Apostle said, "You (i.e. Muslims) will fight with the Jews till some of them will hide behind stones. The stones will (betray them) saying, 'O 'Abdullah (i.e. slave of Allah)! There is a Jew hiding behind me; so kill him.'"

4.195: Narrated Anas: The Prophet set out for Khaibar and reached it at night. He used not to attack if he reached the people at night, till the day broke. So, when the day dawned, the Jews came out with their bags and spades. When they saw the Prophet, they said, "Muhammad and his army!" The Prophet said, "Allahu Akbar! (Allah is Greater) and Khaibar is ruined, for whenever we approach a nation (i.e. enemy to fight) then it will be a miserable morning for those who have been warned."

4.196: Narrated Abu Huraira: Allah's Apostle said, "I have been ordered to fight with the people till they say, 'None has the right to be worshipped but Allah,' and whoever says, 'None has the right to be worshipped but Allah,' his life and property will be saved by me except for Islamic law, and his accounts will be with Allah, (either to punish him or to forgive him.)"

4.199: Narrated Ka'b bin Malik: The Prophet set out on Thursday for the Battle of Tabuk. He used to prefer to set out on Thursdays.

4.248: Narrated 'Abdullah bin 'Amr: A man came to the Prophet asking his permission to take part in Jihad. The Prophet asked him, "Are your parents alive?" He replied in the affirmative. The Prophet said to him, "Then exert yourself in their service."

4.257: Narrated 'Abdullah: During some of the Ghazawat of the Prophet a woman was found killed. Allah's Apostle disapproved the killing of women and children.

4.259: Narrated Abu Huraira: Allah's Apostle sent us in a mission (i.e. an army unit) and said, "If you find so-and-so and so-and-so, burn both of them with fire." When we intended to depart, Allah's Apostle said, "I have ordered you to burn so-and-so and so-and-so, and it is none but Allah Who punishes with fire, so, if you find them, kill them."

4.260: Narrated 'Ikrima: 'Ali burnt some people and this news reached Ibn 'Abbas, who said, "Had I been in his place I would not have burnt them, as the Prophet said, 'Don't punish (anybody) with Allah's Punishment.' No doubt, I would have killed them, for the Prophet said, 'If somebody (a Muslim) discards his religion, kill him.'"

4.261: Narrated Anas bin Malik: A group of eight men from the tribe of 'Ukil came to the Prophet and then they found the climate of Medina unsuitable for them. So, they said, "O Allah's Apostle! Provide us with some milk." Allah's Apostle said, "I recommend that you should join the herd of camels." So they went and drank the urine and the milk of the camels (as a medicine) till they became healthy and fat. Then they killed the shepherd and drove away the camels, and they became unbelievers after they were Muslims. When the Prophet was informed by a shouter for help, he sent some men in their pursuit, and before the sun rose high, they were brought, and he had their hands and feet cut off. Then he ordered for nails which were heated and passed over their eyes, and they were left in the Harra (i.e. rocky land in Medina). They asked for water, and nobody provided them with water till they died. (Abu Qilaba, a sub-narrator said, "They committed murder and theft and fought against Allah and His Apostle, and spread evil in the land.")

4.265: Narrated Al-Bara bin Azib: Allah's Apostle sent a group of the Ansar to Abu Rafi'. 'Abdullah bin Atik entered his house at night and killed him while he was sleeping.

4.268: Narrated Abu Huraira: Allah's Apostle called, "War is deceit."

4.271: Narrated Jabir: The Prophet said, "Who is ready to kill Ka'b bin Ashraf (i.e. a Jew)?" Muhammad bin Maslama replied, "Do you like me to kill him?" The Prophet replied in the affirmative. Muhammad bin Maslama said, "Then allow me to say what I like." The Prophet replied, "I do (i.e. allow you)."

4.280: Narrated Abu Sa'id Al-Khudri: When the tribe of Bani Quraiza was ready to accept Sa'd's judgment, Allah's Apostle sent for Sa'd who was near to him. Sa'd came, riding a donkey and when he came near, Allah's Apostle said (to the Ansar), "Stand up for your leader." Then Sa'd came and sat beside Allah's Apostle who said to him, "These people are ready to accept your judgment." Sa'd said, "I give the judgment that their warriors should be killed and their children and women should be taken as prisoners." The Prophet then remarked, "O Sa'd! You have judged amongst them with (or similar to) the judgment of the King Allah."

4.286: Narrated Salama bin Al-Akwa': "An infidel spy came to the Prophet while he was on a journey. The spy sat with the companions of the Prophet and started talking and then went away. The Prophet said (to his companions), 'Chase and kill him.' So, I killed him." The Prophet then gave him the belongings of the killed spy (in addition to his share of the war booty).

4.300: Narrated Abu Talha: Whenever the Prophet conquered some people, he would stay in their town for three days.

APPENDIX C

WHAT IS THE CALIPHATE?

ALTHOUGH THE CALIPHATE has been an aspiration for many Muslims in the past century, it has been especially prominent in the news since ISIS proclaimed Abu Bakr al-Baghdadi as the caliph and the worldwide leader of all Muslims.

Traditionally, the caliph is the head of the Muslims. According to Sunnis, the first four caliphs were called *rashidun*, or the "rightly guided" caliphs. These were Muhammad's immediate successors: Abu Bakr, Umar, Uthman, and Ali. The fourth caliph, Ali, is a point of extreme controversy. Some Muslims believe that he, being Muhammad's cousin and next of kin, ought to have been the leader immediately after the death of Muhammad. These Muslims are the Shia, and they see Ali as the first imam.

Thus tradition traces the schism between Sunni and Shia to the institution of the caliphate. Today, approximately 80 percent of the Muslim world is Sunni, and 10–15 percent is Shia. The remaining 5–10 percent are a variety of minor sects and denominations, such was the sect to which I belonged.

The caliph has not always been universally recognized even

by Sunnis, particularly since the Mongol invasion of Baghdad in 1258 AD. Shortly after the dissolution of the Ottoman Empire, despite a degree of popularity among Muslims, the caliphate was finally abolished in 1923.

Since then, many Muslims envision the caliphate with nostalgia, hearkening back to the Golden Age of Islam as discussed in Question 6. There can be no caliph now, according to many Muslims, because no nation-state truly represents an Islamic state. As discussed in Question 7, many feel that the Muslim rulers are sycophants to Western leaders, abandoning true sharia for the dream of modernization or perhaps even financial rewards. Many believe this is true even of those nations that purport to adhere to sharia, such as Saudi Arabia and Afghanistan.

When a true Islamic state comes, according to many Muslims, then the institution of the caliphate can be reinstated, and the Muslims of the world will be able to reunite under that banner once more. That is the sentiment that drives ISIS, and that resonates with many young Muslims who have been flocking to Syria and Iraq.

They are not alone. According to Sean Oliver-Dee, a research fellow and scholar at Oxford University in England, "A poll of Muslims in Egypt, Pakistan, Morocco and Indonesia in 2007 found that 65 percent of those interviewed desired to unify all Muslim countries into a single Muslim state; a caliphate." He points out that young Muslims are particularly drawn to an international community, as "a UK poll in 2010 found that 33 percent of Muslims under the age of twenty-four supported a worldwide Islamic caliphate based upon *shari'a* law."

For more information on the caliphate, I recommend Sean Oliver-Dee's booklet *The Caliphate*, or his far more detailed and scholastic *The Caliphate Question*.

APPENDIX D

AHMADI MUSLIMS AND DETAILS ABOUT MY FORMER SECT OF ISLAM

IN THE COURSE OF THIS BOOK I mentioned that I was part of a particular sect of Islam, which was Ahmadiyyat. Many Muslims consider it a heterodox sect, outside the fold of Islam. I believe this conclusion is quite problematic, and that Ahmadis are certainly Muslim.

My position is simple: Ahmadis are Muslims because they believe and proclaim the *shahada*, "There is no god but Allah, and Muhammad is his Messenger." That was the necessary and sufficient requirement as delineated by the traditions of Muhammad and that Muslims follow even today. Muhammad went so far as to say that anyone who says the *shahada* cannot be excommunicated no matter what, according to Sunan Abu Daud, hadith number 2526. But in addition to meeting the necessary and sufficient requirement, Ahmadis also practice the Five Pillars of Islam and believe the Six Articles of Faith, putting them very close to Sunni orthodoxy, closer by far than some other Muslims such as some Sufis. The Ahmadi practice of Islam is virtually indistinguishable from most other Sunnis.

Regardless, some people are concerned about the Muslim charge that Ahmadis are not Muslims. Here is what I hope to convey in this short appendix:

1. The criticism that "Ahmadis aren't Muslim" is a partisan and fundamentalist view, much like Sunnis that call Shia non-Muslim, or Catholics who call Protestants non-Christian, etc.

2. The simplistic view that "Ahmadis aren't Muslim" is an unsophisticated understanding of individuals. My life is an example of a more multi-textured reality than such a monochromatic view allows.

3. Although I believe that Ahmadis are a subgroup of Muslims, and by rejecting Islam I also rejected Ahmadiyyat, I had additional concerns about that particular sect that I ultimately never did investigate.

PARTISAN POLEMICS

Intra-religious rhetoric can often be fierce. Within Christianity, for example, the polemics between Catholics and Protestants have raged since the time of the Reformation into the twenty-first century. The same is true for Islam, and evidence indicates that Muslims around the world are prone to accuse one another of being non-Muslim.

The Pew Research Center published the results of a survey in August 2012, titled "The World's Muslims: Unity and Diversity," demonstrating that Muslims differ drastically on whom they consider Muslim, and their opinions appear to be subjective, dependent upon region and proximity. For example, Muslims disagree on whether Sufis ought to be considered part of the fold: only 24 percent of Muslims in Southeast Asia believed Sufis are Muslims, contrasted with 77 percent of respondents in South Asia.

Of course, the most well-known example of intra-Islamic discord is among Sunni and Shia Muslims. The same survey demonstrated that, out of the five Muslim countries surveyed in the Middle East–North Africa with Sunni majorities, all five of them are very divided as to whether Shia are actually Muslim. In Egypt, Jordan, Morocco, Palestinian Territories, and Tunisia, 40 percent or more of Sunnis think Shia are non-Muslim.

But where Sunnis live among many Shia, their views differ. According to the survey results, "Only in Lebanon and Iraq—nations where sizable populations of Sunnis and Shias live side by side—do large majorities of Sunnis recognize Shias as fellow Muslims."

I noticed a similar phenomenon in our lives as Ahmadi Muslims: when we moved to new areas and met Muslims who did not personally know Ahmadis, they started by treating us as outsiders. But as they got to know us, their view of Ahmadis usually changed. We lived like them, believed like them, and contributed to the community with them. Despite denominational differences, they invariably started to accept us as Muslims when they got to know us.

Since the reasons for including or rejecting sects are often subjective, we ought to acknowledge that the matter of religious inclusion is multifaceted, especially in Islam today. It often has little to do with what people actually believe and how they live, instead dependent on familiarity and proximity. We must be careful not to get embroiled in the partisan polemics.

An example of such polemics that I have often heard argued against Ahmadis is a parallel between Mormonism and Ahmadiyyat: "Mormons call themselves Christian, but they are not really Christian. Similarly, Ahmadis call themselves Muslim but they are not really Muslim." This is a false parallel. Mormonism is generally excluded from Christianity because it is a polytheistic faith, teaching that Jesus is one of many gods. It contravenes a central tenet of Christianity: monotheism. Ahmadiyyat does not deny any central tenets of Islam.

Ahmadiyyat is often accused of heresy because its founder, Mirza Ghulam Ahmad, claimed to be a prophet. Since the Quran says Muhammad is the "seal of the prophets," orthodox Muslims consider Ahmadis to be heretics and non-Muslims. However, as Ahmadis, we were taught that Ahmad was a subordinate prophet, not nearly of the caliber of Muhammad himself. Ahmadis believe Muhammad was the seal of the prophets since he was the last prophet sent with a law; the only degree to which Ahmad had prophetic authority was insofar as he pointed his followers back to Muhammad.

In response to this, I have heard Muslims say that Ahmad himself taught otherwise, but even if that were true, we were never taught anything else. We believed that Muhammad was our ultimate human authority, and Ahmad was simply directing us back to him. Thus, I saw the whole issue of Ahmad's "prophethood" as a semantic one. Regardless, these matters are definitely peripheral issues, as disagreement over the precise interpretation of one verse does not constitute transgression of central Muslim tenets. Ahmadis unquestionably follow and believe the core practices and teachings of Islam.

As I have recently learned, a high court in India concluded that Ahmadis are Muslims for almost exactly the same reasons as mine. In the 1970 case *Shihabuddin Imbichi Koya Thangal vs K.P. Ahmed Koya*, the judge concluded: "The bond of union, if I may say so, consists in the identity of its doctrines, creeds, formularies and tests which are its very core and constitute its distinctive existence. Looking at the issue devoid of sentiment and passion and in the cold light of the law I have no hesitation to hold that the Ahmadiyya sect is of Islam and not alien."

It is noteworthy that this conclusion was drawn by a court in Kerala, India. Kerala is a highly Catholic region of the country, and India itself is overwhelmingly Hindu. This court appeared to have no vested interest in either party, and concluded that Ahmadis are Muslim with "no hesitation."

In fact, this conclusion was based in part on a precedent, when another judge in India, J. Oldfield, concluded similarly regarding Ahmadis. Oldfield's reasoning was based on yet another case, in which the prevailing Muslim denomination charged Wahhabis of not being Muslim, an example of intra-religious polemics that Muslims have since moved past.

The fact of the matter is Muslims have called each other non-Muslim around the world for centuries. Perhaps this is because Muslims have a very narrow view of variety allowed in Islam. The same Pew survey demonstrated that, "In thirty-two of the thirty-nine countries surveyed, half or more Muslims say there is only one correct way to understand the teachings of Islam." The corollary is obvious: such Muslims see any divergence in Islam as heretical.

Currently, Ahmadis are facing scrutiny in most regions, but other regions have already come around: in Bangladesh, for example, the Pew Forum survey found that 40 percent of Sunnis believed Ahmadis to be Muslim. Whatever their reasoning, their conclusion is correct, as Ahmadis fulfill the criteria of inclusion given by the traditions of Muhammad and observed throughout history.

THE COMPLEX TEXTURES OF LIFE

I am often asked questions which attempt to put people into neat boxes, but that is not how life works. For example, many Protestants have asked me whether I think Catholics are Christian. My response is: "Some are and some are not. The same is true of Baptists, Methodists, Anglicans, Seventh Day Adventists, etc." Denominational affiliation often tells us very little about individuals, and painting everyone with the same brush is dangerous.

In my case, although I was an Ahmadi Muslim, I spent the majority of my Muslim life attending a Sunni mosque in Norfolk, Virginia. In fact I hesitate to say that it was a Sunni mosque because there were many denominations there. There was a time when I took religious education courses through that mosque, and my Quran teacher was a Zaidi Shia. So, as an Ahmadi, I was learning the Quran under a Shia teacher employed by a Sunni mosque. That is what Islam looks like in the United States, much more inclusive and diverse than elsewhere in the world. We did not focus on denominational differences.

From the age of ten until my conversion at twenty-two, I

often fasted with Sunnis and Shias at that mosque, celebrated Eid festivals, gathered at their homes, and otherwise was a part of the community. Perhaps the greatest indication that I was integrated into the Muslim community was that I prayed salaat with them, usually being led by them but at times even leading prayers at peoples' homes as the imam myself. Many Ahmadis do not pray behind non-Ahmadis, but when I reached adulthood and discovered their reasoning, I found it very problematic. I did not have anything against praying with other Muslims, seeing myself as one of them, and so I often did.

MY ASSESSMENT OF AHMADIYYAT WHILE MUSLIM

When I was investigating Islam and Christianity, my position was rather simple: since Ahmadiyyat is a subgroup of Islam, I would investigate its evidence after investigating the evidence for Islam. If there were good reason to believe in Islam, then I would investigate its various denominations. However, if Islam proved to be historically problematic, then there would be no need to consider any of its denominations. As it turned out, the latter was my conclusion. On account of the evidence, I rejected the *shahada*, and in so doing I rejected Ahmadiyyat.

That said, I had come across some troubling matters regarding Ahmadiyyat before rejecting Islam. While I was researching Islam and Christianity, a close childhood friend of mine rejected Ahmadiyyat for Sunni Islam. Intrigued, I asked him his reasons, and he shared many arguments with me that I thought, if true, would pose significant problems for Ahmadiyyat.

For instance, he argued that Mirza Ghulam Ahmad had issued many false prophecies. An example he gave was that Ahmad had prophesied that he would live until the age of eighty, but he died about a decade before that. Another of his failed prophecies was that a certain woman would marry him; she never did marry Ahmad, and a great controversy resulted on account of the failed prophecy. My friend also suggested that Ahmad had defrauded hundreds of people; he pledged to write fifty books for them and took payment for all fifty up front, but ultimately only wrote five. He justified this by saying, essentially, "The difference between 'fifty' and 'five' is a zero, and since zero is nothing, I have delivered what I promised."

These were just three of dozens of reasons my friend left Ahmadiyyat for Sunni Islam. I knew of a handful of other people that left Ahmadiyyat for other reasons, including the accusation that Ahmadiyyat functioned as a cult, with strong central control and a tendency to excommunicate people even for minor transgressions, such as playing music at weddings. But, as before, I had decided to visit these matters more carefully only if I determined Islam was true, and that never happened.

CONCLUSION

In the end, I think it is important to recognize that the grey areas make it difficult to draw boundaries of religious inclusion and identity. If inclusion in a religion were based on majority opinion, then Ahmadis would not be Muslim, but Sufis would not be either, nor would Shias be Muslim in some places, and Sunnis would be excluded in others. Such a measure ultimately becomes absurd.

That is why I suggest religious identity be determined by those beliefs and practices that distinguished a community from its surroundings during its inception. At the inception of Islam, what made someone a Muslim was whether he assented to the authoritative prophethood of Muhammad and exclusively worshiped the one god Allah. I think that all who do so today are Muslim, including Ahmadis. Most importantly, Muhammad suggested the same.

But whether someone agrees with me or not, the fact remains that this book investigates Islam and speaks to the common Muslim experience. It is my prayer that the reader of this book will not be deterred by partisan polemics.

GLOSSARY

Abrogation—In Islam, the doctrine of abrogation, or cancelling, refers to a portion of the Quran being cancelled. The term can mean that a passage has been taken out of the book, or that the command of a verse has been rescinded, or both.

Badr—The first of the five major battles fought by the Muslims, it was a result of a Muslim raid against a Meccan caravan during which, against the odds, Muslims succeeded in defeating their opponents.

Bidah—In Islam, a teaching or practice that is not original to the foundational texts of Islam. The term literally means "innovation," and it is a negative term implying inauthenticity.

Burqa—The outer garments a Muslim woman wears in accordance with Quranic commands of modesty.

Dabiq—The field of battle where many Muslims believe Armageddon will begin. Also the name of ISIS's glossy magazine.

Dar al-Harb—The "House of War," a term for lands that did not belong to Muslims or those with whom the Muslims had a treaty.

Dar al-Islam—The "House of Islam," or the lands of the Muslims.

Dar al-Sulh—The "House of Treaty," or lands that belonged to those with whom the Muslims had agreed not to fight.

Dhimmi—A protected, second-class citizen living under Muslim rule.

Fiqh—The application of *sharia* in the lives of Muslims.

Ghilman—A term for slave soldiers of the early Muslims, starting around the ninth century.

Hadith—A tradition of something Muhammad has said. These are often accompanied with chains of transmission, or authorities that recounted the tradition tracing back to Muhammad himself. The term *hadith* also functions as an umbrella term for *sunnah*, the actions of Muhammad recorded in tradition.

Hijaz—An expanse of land on the west side of Arabia on the Red Sea, encompassing the important Muslim cities of Mecca, Medina, and modern day Jeddah.

Hypocrites—A category of Muslims in the Quran who proclaim to follow Muhammad and Allah, but who do not do so in reality. They incur harsh judgment from Allah, and the warnings given to them seem intended to make all Muslims more zealous for their religion.

Ijma—A consensus of Muslim jurists.

Ijtihad—The process of jurisprudence in sharia.

Islam—The religion of Muslims, traditionally understood to have been established by Muhammad in 610 AD. The word itself means "surrender."

Islamic fundamentalist—A nebulous term that has been defined by some to mean those Muslims who support the implementation of Islamic law and, by extension, other beliefs and practices that are considered antiquated by modern standards.

Jahiliyya—An Islamic term for pre-Islamic days, evoking imagery of illiteracy and barbarity.

Jihad—A word meaning "struggle," it ultimately came to describe the Muslim doctrine of spiritual warfare. It can be used spiritually, but in the traditions of Muhammad's life and in the Quran it is primarily used for fighting.

Jizya—The ransom tax that dhimmis had to pay Muslims in order to live in their lands. This gave them a protected, second-class status.

Khybar—A Jewish stronghold that was decimated by Muhammad and maintains a significant place in the memory of radical Muslims today.

Mamluk—A term for slave soliders of the classical Islamic era, starting around the eleventh century.

Nakhla—The first successful raid of the Muslims, it was conducted on the order of Muhammad during the Arab holy month of truce, resulting in great controversy.

Purdah—The practice of Muslim women to keep themselves veiled.

Qiyas—Analogical reasoning, used in Islamic jurisprudence.

Quran—The Muslim holy scriptures, serving as the foundation for sharia and the primary proclamation of Muhammad.

Ramadan—The Muslim holy month, wherein fasting is mandatory, among other Islamic traditions.

Glossary

Salafi—Muslims who attempt to follow the first generations of Muslims, the "ancestors," in their strict adherence to Islamic practice. This fundamentalist devotion often results in violent expressions of Islam.

Shahada—The proclamation that "there is no god but Allah, and Muhammad is his Messenger." It is the motto of all Muslims, and reciting it with true belief is sufficient for conversion to Islam.

Sharia—Technically translated "path to water," it is the term for Islamic law, encompassing the proper way to live life for a Muslim.

Shia—A branch of Islam that envisions succession of Islamic leadership to have proceeded by Muhammad's bloodline rather than election. They constitute approximately 10–15 percent of Muslims worldwide.

Shirk—The unforgivable sin in Islam, associating partners with Allah. This is analogous to blasphemy, and it includes such things as worshiping stones or worshiping Jesus.

Sufi—An order of Muslims sometimes distinct from the branches of Sunni or Shia. Their expression of Islam is often less focused on legalities and traditions, and relatively more focused on spiritual and ethical matters.

Sunnah—The actions of Muhammad recorded in Islamic tradition.

Sunni—The majority branch of Islam, constituting approximately 80 percent of Muslims worldwide.

Takbir—The Islamic slogan Allahu Akbar, which means "Allah is greater." It is a versatile phrase, used for many purposes. The traditions show Muhammad using it in celebration, in glorification of Allah, and in intimidation of his enemies.

Takfir—The Islamic doctrine of excommunication. Classically, Muslims have been very inclusive of other Muslims, a tradition that traces back to Muhammad. Radical Muslims, however, use this doctrine to justify their attacks on less zealous Muslims that they consider hypocrites.

Tawhid—The Islamic doctrine of God, formulated partially in response to the Trinity. It is the proclamation of an absolutely monadic God.

Ummah—The worldwide population of the Muslim people, seen as one.

Sneak Peek

The following is an excerpt from Nabeel Qureshi's forthcoming book, No God but One: Allah or Jesus?

PROLOGUE

FATIMA'S DILEMMA

"Repent! Otherwise you have blasphemed!"

Her brother had seethed with rage, and his words still echoed in Fatima's mind. *Repent! You have blasphemed!* The words were laced with threat: The penalty for blasphemy was death. Had she really blasphemed? She hadn't meant to. It had been a heated argument; she had accidentally blurted out some words. But what now? How could this have happened? She was struggling to think clearly. Her very life was in jeopardy.

Lifting her face from her hands, Fatima glanced at her computer. Her computer! It was where she had confided her most private thoughts and inner struggles, where she could discuss new ideas and share opinions with compassionate ears. Her computer was her window to friends and freedom.

But not this day. This day, it had betrayed her. As a result, she had been locked in her room for hours and feared for her life. Her brother could return at any moment, and unless she repented, it could be the end. She had to think. She had to think quickly and clearly.

Despite its treachery, her computer remained her only recourse. As she had so many times before, she returned to her laptop to help her process. Logging on to an Arabic forum, she began a post.

Timestamp: 5:15 A.M., July 24, 2008
Author: Rania

She had been signing on for years as Rania, but the forum knew her well. They knew that she was really twenty-six-year-old Sara Fatima al-Mutairi, a spirited young woman, passionate teacher, patriotic Saudi, and recent convert to Christianity.

She was born in the province of Qasim. Her family came from a distinguished Bedouin tribe and raised Fatima in accordance with their ancestral religion of Islam. Desiring a devout daughter, her mother had enrolled her in a Quran school at a young age, and Fatima began to take her Islamic faith very seriously. She started learning the Quran, then scrupulously covering her hair with her hijab and even fasting twice a week. She began to outstrip her family in religious zeal, avoiding television and secular music, ultimately giving up her friends in her fervor.

Fatima's mother grew concerned. She desired a faithful daughter, not a fanatical one. This was not the Islam she knew. Regretting her decision, she took Fatima out of the Quran school and enrolled her in the state system.

Over the years, Fatima's life normalized, yet she maintained a passion for her religion. She engaged in online debates with agnostics and apostates, defending her beloved prophet and religion from their attacks. She investigated Islamic history and theology carefully, confident her faith would stand up to scrutiny. But in the course of these debates, she realized, with anguish and despair, that she could no longer follow Islam. She stopped eating for several days, fell into depression, and became an atheist.

But something told her this wasn't the answer. She began her search for God anew, this time calling out to him for help. It was then that she came across the Gospels, particularly the gospel of Matthew. It captivated her. She read it four times, being most moved by the Sermon on the Mount. After much investigation and deliberation, she accepted its message. The Christian community with which she connected advised her to keep her new faith a secret, because in Arabia, those who leave Islam incur the penalty of death. This was difficult for Fatima, passionate and outspoken as she was, but she hid her conversion from all, keeping her private thoughts on her computer and conversing with her Christian community only online.

It was to this online community that she now returned in her moment of despair. After brief thought, she titled her post and continued:

> Timestamp: 5:15 A.M., July 24, 2008
> Author: Rania
> Title: I am in big trouble
> Body: The peace of our Lord and our God and Jesus the Messiah. I am in big trouble. My family has started to doubt me because of a religious argument this evening with my mother and brother.

Her brother. Fatima did not need to explain to the forum how dangerous an argument with him could be. Fatima's brother had had a similar start in the same family, but his story progressed very differently. His fervor for Islam had only grown since childhood. He did become fanatical. Ultimately he joined the Commission for the Promotion of Virtue and the Prevention of Vice, Saudi Arabia's religious police, dedicated to enforcing a stringent version of Islam upon its citizens. Although many Muslims take issue with the commission and with Saudi Arabia's dogmatic version of Islam in general, the commission's religious stringency attracts zealous young men like Fatima's brother.

Fatima's fingers flew across the keyboard, the words now pouring out of her as she recounted the harrowing events of the evening. She explained that in a moment of weakness, she had complained about her lack of religious freedom in Islam. When her family pressed her to explain herself, she had blurted, "The way of the Messiah is purer than the way of the Messenger, and there is a great difference between them!" Her brother flew into a rage, threatening. Even though Fatima tried to apologize, he broke into her room, took her computer, and searched her files. There he found Fatima's journals, her Christian confessions, and even a picture of the cross. His suspicions were confirmed. Malice flooded his eyes. He left her, giving her four hours to reconsider what she had done.

As she came to the end of her post, she made a simple request: "His glance frightened me. I do not trust him. Pray for me, please."

Four hours had passed. The time had come. Her brother would return at any moment. She had to choose: Would she repent and embrace Islam, or would she stand firm in her Christian faith, potentially at the cost of her life? Which would it be, Islam or Christianity?

ISLAM OR CHRISTIANITY?

For Fatima, absolutely everything hinged on that question. No matter the strength of her convictions, when faced with the threat of death, she no doubt had a moment of considering how certain she really was: "Is the way of the Messiah truly all that different from the way of the Messenger? Can we really be confident that one religion or the other is true? Even so, is the truth worth dying for?"

Every year, millions are faced with Fatima's decision: to follow Islam or Christianity, to worship Allah or Jesus. Like Fatima, unless the seeker lives in a nominal or secular environment, the stakes are high: It can cost a seeker her family, her friends, her job, and her life. For such seekers, it's not simply a matter of believing whatever seems right. They need to be sure, and they need to be sure it's worth the sacrifice.

For me, it has been a decade since I left Islam, and the fallout of my decision haunts me every day. I knew it would, well before I ever converted, but I also knew that I was sure. I was sure that Islam and Christianity are not just two paths that lead to the same God but two very different paths that teach very different things about God. I was sure that I had excellent historical reasons to believe the gospel. I was sure that though I loved Islam, I couldn't ignore the problems that plagued its foundations.

But most of all, I was sure that following the one true God would be worth all trials and all suffering. I had to follow the evidence and the truth, no matter the cost.

I left my religion of twenty-two years and became a follower of Jesus in 2005. In 2009, I decided to leave the medical field in order to share what I had learned about the gospel, the message of Christianity. I sincerely believe that this message has the power to transform hearts and change the world. The God it proclaims is unlike any other, and it is an unfathomable honor that we get to be a part of his story and introduce people to him.

While sharing this message, I often come across two kinds of people: Christians who enjoy criticizing Islam, and Muslims who want to argue but do not want to learn. I am not writing this book for either of them. I am writing for people who, like Fatima did, like I did, need the answers to these questions:

1. Are Islam and Christianity all that different?
2. Can we be confident that one religion or the other is true?
3. Is it worth sacrificing everything for the truth?

It took me four years to answer these questions, and they remain so important to me that I studied them for another decade. This book is my brief answer. After I share my findings, we will see how Fatima answered the same questions and discover the outcome of her story.

Get Additional Resources for *Answering Jihad*

Visit NabeelQureshi.com

- Gain access to bonus materials.
- Sign up to receive email updates from Nabeel on new projects.
- Discover new resources for better understanding Christianity, Islam, and their intersection.

No God but One: Allah or Jesus?

A Former Muslim
Investigates the Evidence
for Islam and Christianity

Nabeel Qureshi

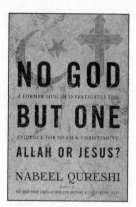

On account of the superficial points
of agreement between Islam and Christianity, many don't
see how tremendously deep the divides between them really are, and fewer still have considered the evidence for
each faith. How is jihad different from the crusades? Can
we know the life of Jesus as well as the life of Muhammad?
What reason is there to believe in one faith over the other,
and what difference can the gospel really make?

In *No God but One: Allah or Jesus?*, *New York Times* best-
selling author Nabeel Qureshi takes readers on a global,
historical, yet deeply personal journey to the heart of the
world's two largest religions. He explores the claims that
each faith makes upon believers' intellects and lives, critically examining the evidence in support of their distinctive
beliefs.

Readers of Qureshi's first book, *Seeking Allah, Finding
Jesus*, will appreciate his careful and respectful comparison
of Islam and Christianity. Both religions teach that there is
no God but one, but who deserves to be worshiped, Allah
or Jesus?

Available in stores and online!

Seeking Allah, Finding Jesus

A Devout Muslim Encounters Christianity

Nabeel Qureshi

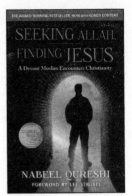

In *Seeking Allah, Finding Jesus*, now expanded with bonus content, Nabeel Qureshi describes his dramatic journey from Islam to Christianity, complete with friendships, investigations, and supernatural dreams along the way.

Engaging and thought provoking, *Seeking Allah, Finding Jesus* tells a powerful story of the clash between Islam and Christianity in one man's heart and of the peace he eventually found in Jesus.

Available in stores and online!